AMERICAN THiNK

STUDENT'S BOOK 1

Herbert Puchta, Jeff Stranks & Peter Lewis-Jones

CAMBRIDGE
UNIVERSITY PRESS

CONTENTS

PRONUNCIATION	THINK	SKILLS	
/s/, /z/, /ɪz/ sounds	**Values:** Taking care of yourself **Self esteem:** Why it's good to have a hobby	Reading	Quiz: Do you take good care of yourself? Blog: What do you do in your free time? Photostory: Olivia's new hobby
		Writing	Writing about routines
		Listening	Conversations about hobbies
Contractions	**Values:** Fashion and clothes **Train to Think:** Exploring numbers	Reading	Soap opera: Shopping Web chat: How not to spend money Culture: World markets
		Writing	An informal email to say what you're doing
		Listening	Shopping dialogues
Vowel sounds: /ɪ/ and /i/	**Values:** Food and health **Self esteem:** Being happy	Reading	Article: Food facts or food fiction? Blog: My brother's cooking Photostory: The picnic
		Writing	An email about your favorite or least favorite meal
		Listening	Ordering food in a café
Saying -er	**Values:** TV families **Train to Think:** Making inferences	Reading	Article: TV families Article: The swimming pool heroes Culture: Around the world on Children's Day
		Writing	An invitation
		Listening	Why my family drives me crazy
Regular past tense endings: /d/, /t/, /ɪd/	**Values:** Community spirit **Self esteem:** Feeling safe	Reading	Article: The LEGO house Blog: Dad gets it right! (finally) Photostory: Hey, look at that guy!
		Writing	Summary of a text; blog post
		Listening	What is "home"?
Stressed syllables in words	**Values:** Friendship and loyalty **Train to Think:** Making decisions	Reading	Article: Best friends … 8,000 miles apart Article: How we met Culture: Friendship myths
		Writing	An apology
		Listening	A story about Cristiano Ronaldo
Vowel sounds: /ʊ/ and /u/	**Values:** Caring for people and the environment **Self esteem:** Classroom rules	Reading	Article: "… just because I didn't want to take a bath" Website: Product reviews Photostory: The treasure hunt
		Writing	A paragraph about housework
		Listening	Radio program – advice for young inventors
Stress in numbers	**Values:** Giving your time to others **Train to Think:** Creative thinking	Reading	Article: Mary gives everything for Teen Feed! Text messages: At the airport Culture: Volunteering abroad
		Writing	A blog entry about volunteering
		Listening	Interviews about how people spend time
Vowel sounds: /ɪ/ and /aɪ/	**Values:** Valuing our world **Self esteem:** Being brave	Reading	Article: An amazing place Article: Could you live there? Photostory: The competition
		Writing	An email about a place
		Listening	Interview with a Kalahari Bushman
Voiced /ð/ and unvoiced /θ/ consonants	**Values:** Appreciating other cultures **Train to Think:** Problem solving	Reading	Blogs: Alice's World; The Life of Brian Letters to a newspaper: Our Town: What's wrong and what can we do about it? Culture: Ghost towns around the world
		Writing	An informal email
		Listening	A conversation between people arranging to go out
The /h/ consonant sound	**Values:** Exercise and health **Self esteem:** Getting help	Reading	Article: Changing bodies Web chats: Crazy things that parents say to their kids Photostory: The phone call
		Writing	A phone message
		Listening	Dialogues about physical problems
Sentence stress	**Values:** Travel broadens the mind **Train to Think:** Exploring differences	Reading	Blog: The non-stop traveler Interview: The taxi driver Culture: Hard journeys for schoolchildren
		Writing	An essay about someone you admire
		Listening	A traveler talking to children at his old school

WELCOME

A ALL ABOUT ME
Personal information

1 🔊 1.02 **Put the dialogue in order. Number the boxes. Listen and check.**

1	a	ALEX	Hi. I'm Alex.
	b	ALEX	I'm 14. How about you?
	c	ALEX	The U.K.
	d	ALEX	Hello, Daniela. Where are you from?
	e	DANIELA	Me? I'm 14, too.
	f	DANIELA	I'm from Mexico. And you?
	g	DANIELA	Hi, Alex. My name's Daniela.
	h	DANIELA	Cool! How old are you, Alex?

2 🔊 1.03 **Complete the dialogue with the phrases in the list. Listen and check.**

are | meet | this | too

ALEX Daniela, ¹_____ is my friend Kei.

KEI Hi, Daniela. Nice to ²_____ you.

DANIELA Nice to meet you, ³_____ , Kei.
And this is my friend. Her name's Maria.

MARIA Hi, guys. How ⁴_____ you? I'm Maria.
Maria Hernandez.

3 SPEAKING **Imagine you are a famous person. Work in pairs, then groups.**

1 Tell your partner who you are.

2 Introduce your partner to others in the group.

> Hi, I'm Ryan Gosling.

> Hello, my name's Rihanna. And this is my friend, Barack Obama.

Nationalities and *be*

4 **Complete the names of the countries (add the consonants).**

1 _ _ a _ i _

2 the U _ i _ e _ _ _ _ a _ e _

3 _ a _ a _

4 _ o _ o _ _ i a

5 E _ _ ua _ o _

6 _ e _ i _ o

7 _ a _ a _ a

8 _ e _ u

9 _ u _ e _

10 the U _ i _ e _ _ _ i _ _ _ _ o _

11 _ _ i _ a

12 A _ _ e _ _ i _ a

Carlos

0   *He's Brazilian.*

Sandra

1   *She's* _____

Kei and Sarah

2   _____

Carmen and José

3   _____

Ricardo

4   _____

Burcu

5   _____

Emily

6   _____

Alex

7   _____

Andrea

8   _____

Raul and Luis

9   _____

5   **What nationality are the people? Write the sentences.**

6   🔊 1.04 **Complete the dialogue using the correct forms of the verb *to be*. Then listen and check.**

DANIELA   So, Kei – where 0 ___*are*___ you from?

KEI   Me? I 1_____ from the United States. Alex here 2_____ British, but I 3_____ American.

MARIA   But 4_____ your name American?

KEI   Oh, good question. Well, no it 5_____ . My parents 6_____ from Japan and so my name 7_____ from Japan, too. But my sister Sarah and I were both born here, so we 8_____ American.

DANIELA   That 9_____ cool. I think your name 10_____ really nice.

KEI   Thank you! And you two, 11_____ you both Mexican?

MARIA   That 12_____ right. But we 13_____ not from the same city. I 14_____ from Mexico City, and Daniela 15_____ from Monterrey. We 16_____ students at the language school here.

Names and addresses

7   🔊 1.05 **Kei calls for a taxi. Listen and complete the information.**

◆◆◆ COOPER'S TAXIS ◆◆◆

Booking form

Taxi for	1 _____
Going to	2 _____
Pick up at	3 _____ a.m./p.m.
From	4 _____ Street
Number of passengers	5 _____

8   🔊 1.06 **Now listen to a phone call. Correct each of these sentences.**

0   Alex calls Maria.
    No — Maria calls Alex.

1   They met last Wednesday.

2   There's a party at Maria's place next Friday.

3   The party starts at 7:30.

4   Maria lives at 134 Markam Avenue.

5   Her phone number is 946-814-6305.

B WHAT'S THAT?
Things in the classroom

1 Match the words in the list with the things in the pictures.

board [2]   book [ ]   CD [ ]   chair [ ]   desk [ ]   floor [ ]
pen [ ]   pencil [ ]   ruler [ ]   window [ ]   door [ ]   notebook [ ]

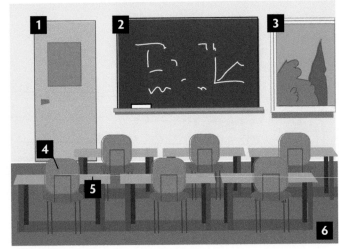 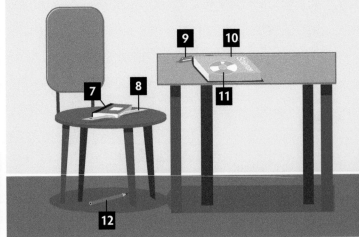

Prepositions of place

2 Look at the pictures. Complete each sentence with a preposition from the list (you will use some words more than once).

on | between | in | under | in front of | behind

0 The notebook is _____*on*_____ the chair.
1 The pencil is _____ the floor.
2 The pencil is _____ the chair.
3 The pen is _____ the book.
4 The ruler is _____ the notebook.
5 The board is _____ the door and the window.
6 The book is _____ the pen.

Classroom language

3 🔊 1.07 Complete each sentence with a word from the list. Listen and check.

ask | again | mean | hand | don't
page | me | say | spell | understand

1 Excuse _____ .
2 Can I _____ a question, please?
3 Can you say that _____ , please?
4 How do you _____ *cansado* in English?
5 Open your books to _____ 21.
6 Raise your _____ if you know the answer.
7 Sorry, I _____ know.
8 Sorry, I don't _____ .
9 What does the word "ordinary" _____ ?
10 Excuse me. How do you _____ that word? Is it T-I-R-E-D or T-Y-R-E-D?

4 🔊 1.08 Use one of the sentences in Exercise 3 to complete each mini-dialogue. Listen and check.

1 TEACHER   Good morning, everyone.
  STUDENTS   Good morning.
  TEACHER   OK. Let's start. _____

2 TEACHER   So, Michael, what's the answer?
  MICHAEL   _____
  TEACHER   That's OK. What about you, Susie?

3 STUDENT   _____ ,
             Mrs. McFarlane. I have a question.
  TEACHER   Yes, what is it?
  STUDENT   _____ "fascinating" _____ ?
  TEACHER   It means "very, very interesting."

5 🔊 1.09 Put the lines in order to make a dialogue. Listen and check.

[ ] A E-N-O-U-G-H.
[ ] A No, that's completely wrong!
[1] A How do you think you spell the word "enough"?
[ ] A No, that's really how you spell it.
[ ] B OK, how do you spell it, then?
[ ] B Oh. Let me think. Is it E-N-U-F-F?
[ ] B You're kidding!

6 SPEAKING Work in pairs. Think of a word in English. Can your partner spell it?

How do you spell "awful"?   *A-W-F-U-L.*

That's right.

Object pronouns

7 Complete each sentence with the correct pronoun.

0 She's a good teacher – we like _her_ a lot.

1 My pens are under your desk. Can you get _____ , please?

2 I have a new book – I'm going to read _____ this afternoon.

3 Sorry, can you speak more loudly? I can't hear _____ .

4 I don't understand our homework – can you help _____ ?

5 He doesn't understand, so please help _____ .

6 We like our teacher. She gives _____ good grades!

this / that / these / those

8 Match the pictures and sentences.

1 What does this word mean?

2 What does that word mean?

3 These books are heavy.

4 Those books are heavy.

9 Complete the email by writing one word in each space.

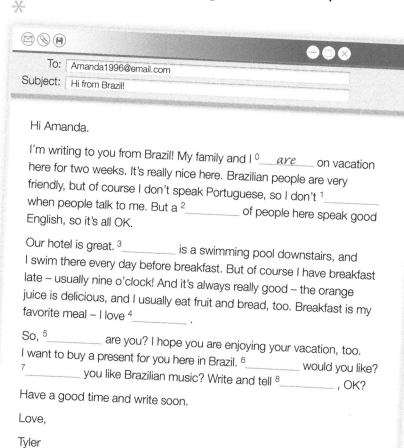

To: Amanda1996@email.com
Subject: Hi from Brazil!

Hi Amanda.

I'm writing to you from Brazil! My family and I [0] _are_ on vacation here for two weeks. It's really nice here. Brazilian people are very friendly, but of course I don't speak Portuguese, so I don't [1] _____ when people talk to me. But a [2] _____ of people here speak good English, so it's all OK.

Our hotel is great. [3] _____ is a swimming pool downstairs, and I swim there every day before breakfast. But of course I have breakfast late – usually nine o'clock! And it's always really good – the orange juice is delicious, and I usually eat fruit and bread, too. Breakfast is my favorite meal – I love [4] _____ .

So, [5] _____ are you? I hope you are enjoying your vacation, too. I want to buy a present for you here in Brazil. [6] _____ would you like? [7] _____ you like Brazilian music? Write and tell [8] _____ , OK?

Have a good time and write soon.

Love,

Tyler

A

B

C

D

C ABOUT TIME
Days and dates

1 🔊 1.10 Listen and (circle) the correct information.

OLIVER   Hi, Lauren. Why are you so happy today?

LAUREN   Because it's February [1]*21st / 22nd / 23rd*.

OLIVER   And what's special about that date?

LAUREN   It's my birthday!

OLIVER   Really! Happy birthday, Lauren.

LAUREN   Thanks. I'm [2]*12 / 13 / 14* today.

OLIVER   Lucky you!

LAUREN   When is your birthday, Oliver?

OLIVER   It's in [3]*August / September / October*.

LAUREN   What date?

OLIVER   The [4]*11th / 12th / 13th*. I think it's on a [5]*Tuesday / Thursday / Friday* this year.

2 🔊 1.11 **Complete the names of the days and months. Listen and check.**

DAYS

1 M o n d a y
2 T _ _ sd _ _ _
3 W _ _ n _ d _ _ _
4 _ h u _ _ _ _ _ y

5 F _ _ _ _ _ _
6 S _ _ _ _ r _ _ _ y
7 S _ _ _ _ _

MONTHS

1 J _ _ u _ _ y
2 F _ bru _ _ _ _
3 M _ _ _ _ h
4 _ p _ _ l
5 M _ _
6 J _ _ _

7 J _ _ _ y
8 A _ _ u _ _
9 S _ _ _ _ _ mber
10 O _ _ _ _ _ _ er
11 _ _ vem _ _ _ _
12 D _ _ _ _ _ _ _ _

3 **Draw lines to match the numbers and the words.**

first	22nd
second	3rd
third	12th
fourth	4th
fifth	15th
twelfth	2nd
fifteenth	5th
twentieth	31st
twenty-second	1st
thirty-first	20th

4 🔊 1.12 **How do you say these numbers? Listen and check.**

7th | 11th | 14th | 19th | 23rd | 28th | 30th

5 🔊 1.13 **Listen and write the people's birthdays.**

1   *August 4th*   2 _____

3 _____   4 _____

5 _____   6 _____

6 [SPEAKING] **Walk around the classroom. Ask and answer questions. Whose birthday is close to your birthday?**

When's your birthday?   *It's on March 18th.*

My day

7 Put the pictures in the order you do them.

A I go to school.

B I get home.

C I go to bed.

D I have dinner.

I have breakfast.
E

F I get up.

G I do my homework.

H I have lunch.

8 Look at the sentences in Exercise 7. Write them in the correct column <u>for you</u>.

Morning	Afternoon	Evening
I get up.		

9 Match the clocks and the times.

1 It's eight thirty.
2 It's a quarter after three.
3 It's eleven o'clock.
4 It's six o'clock.
5 It's eight o'clock.
6 It's a quarter to eight.
7 It's ten to one.
8 It's twenty after ten.

A 2

I *get home.*

B

I _____

C

I _____

D

I _____

E

I _____

F

I _____

G

I _____

H

I _____

> **LOOK!**
>
> midnight to noon = a.m.
> noon to midnight = p.m.
> 12 a.m. = midnight
> 12 p.m. = noon
>
> 1 a.m. = 1 o'clock in the early morning
> 1 p.m. = 1 o'clock in the afternoon

10 🔊 1.14 Listen to Leah. Write about her day under the pictures in Exercise 9.

11 SPEAKING Work in pairs. Talk about your day.

> I get up at seven thirty.

> I have lunch at twelve o'clock.

D MY THINGS
My possessions

1 Read Chloe's blog and check (✓) the photos of the things she has.

2 Work in pairs. Put the things Chloe talks about in the correct category.

PERSONAL POSSESSIONS: _TV_ , _laptop_ , ____, ____, ____, ____

PETS: _cat_ , ____

have

3 Complete the table with *have*, *has*, *don't*, or *doesn't*.

Affirmative	Negative
I have a dog.	I don't have a cat.
You ¹_____ a dog.	You ⁵_____ _____ a cat.
He has a dog.	He doesn't have a cat.
She ²_____ a dog.	She ⁶_____ _____ a cat.
We ³_____ a dog.	We ⁷_____ _____ a cat.
They ⁴_____ a dog.	They ⁸_____ _____ a cat.

Questions	Short answers
Do I have a pet?	Yes, you do. / No, you don't.
⁹_____ you _____ a pet?	Yes, I ¹³_____
	No, I ¹⁴_____
Does he have a pet?	Yes, he does. / No, he doesn't.
¹⁰_____ she _____ a pet?	Yes, she ¹⁵_____
	No, she ¹⁶_____
¹¹_____ we _____ a pet?	Yes, we ¹⁷_____
	No, we ¹⁸_____
¹²_____ they _____ a pet?	Yes, they ¹⁹_____
	No, they ²⁰_____

4 Complete the sentences with *have*, *has*, *don't have*, or *doesn't have* so they are true for you.

1 I _____ a tablet.
2 My dad _____ a computer.
3 I _____ a dog.
4 My best friend _____ a brother.
5 I _____ a TV in my bedroom.
6 My mom _____ a car.

5 **SPEAKING** Walk around the classroom. Find someone who has …

1 a red bike
2 a cat and a dog
3 an English dictionary
4 a website
5 two brothers or sisters
6 a smart phone
7 an unusual pet
8 a house with a garden

Do you have a bike?   *Yes, I do.*

What color is it?

I like and *I'd like*

6 Match the pictures and the sentences.

A

B

C

D

1 I like apples!

2 I'd like a hot shower!

3 I'd like six apples.

4 I like hot showers.

7 🔊 1.15 Complete with *I like* or *I'd like*. Listen and check.

0 A What's your favorite food?

 B *I like* tacos most.

1 A Can I help you?

 B Yes, _____ a kilo of oranges.

2 A _____ ice cream, please.

 B Chocolate or strawberry?

3 A What do you want to watch?

 B Well, _____ movies, so can we watch a movie, please?

4 A _____ riding bikes. Do you?

 B Not much. I think running's better.

5 A Do you want pizza or a burger?

 B Well, pizza's my favorite food – but today, _____ a burger, please!

8 Complete the menu with the words in the list.

banana | orange juice | chicken | cookie

Lunch Menu

Sandwiches:

cheese or ¹_____

Desserts:

cake or ²_____

Fruit:

apple or ³_____

Drinks:

water or ⁴_____

9 🔊 1.16 Listen to the dialogue. What does Max want for lunch? (Circle) the food above.

10 🔊 1.16 Write the questions in the spaces to complete part of the dialogue. Listen again and check.

OK. What fruit would you like?

Do you have bananas?

What would you like for lunch today?

Would you like a chicken sandwich or a cheese sandwich?

LUNCH LADY	Hi, Max. ¹_____
MAX	I'd like a sandwich, please.
LUNCH LADY	²_____
MAX	A cheese sandwich, please.
LUNCH LADY	³_____
MAX	⁴_____
LUNCH LADY	Yes, we do.
MAX	A banana, please.

11 SPEAKING Work in pairs. Make lunch for your partner. Ask and answer questions.

Would you like a ... or ... ?

What ... would you like?

1 | HAVING FUN

A

B

C

E

F

G

D

H

READING

1 Match the activities in the list with the photos. Write 1–8 in the boxes.

1 sleeping	5 reading
2 doing homework	6 dancing
3 playing soccer	7 cleaning
4 studying	8 singing

2 Are these activities fun? Write *always*, *sometimes*, or *never*.

1 Sleeping is _____ fun.
2 Doing homework is _____ fun.
3 Playing soccer is _____ fun.
4 Studying is _____ fun.
5 Reading is _____ fun.
6 Dancing is _____ fun.
7 Cleaning is _____ fun.
8 Singing is _____ fun.

3 **SPEAKING** Work in groups of three and compare your ideas from Exercise 2.

> *I think dancing is always fun.*

> *I think it's sometimes fun.*

4 **SPEAKING** Think of more activities and say what you think.

> *Riding a bike is always fun.*

> *Doing housework is never fun.*

5 🔊 1.17 Read and listen to the quiz. Match the pictures with the questions in the quiz. Write 1–7 in the boxes.

Do you take good care of yourself?

Does your teacher give you a lot of homework? Do your parents always want your bedroom clean? Schoolwork, housework – life isn't always easy. There are a lot of things to do, and there isn't always time to do them. But in your busy life it's important to think about yourself, too. It's important to do things you like, things that make you happy. Everyone needs fun.

So do you take good care of yourself? Take our quiz and find out.

4 How many hours do you sleep a night?
a) nine to ten hours
b) about eight
c) less than eight

5 Do you like to exercise?
a) Yes, exercise is fun.
b) It's OK.
c) No. It's really boring.

6 Do you like puzzles and crosswords?
a) I love them.
b) They're OK.
c) I don't really like them. They're boring.

1 Do you smile a lot?
a) Yes, I smile all the time.
b) I only smile when I'm happy.
c) My best friend says I don't smile very often.

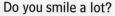

2 How many hobbies do you have?
a) I have lots of hobbies.
b) One or two.
c) I don't have any hobbies.

3 When do you relax?
a) In the morning, afternoon, and evening.
b) I relax when I have time.
c) I never relax. I'm always busy.

7 Which of these things do you do most?
a) Talk with friends and family.
b) Meet friends online.
c) Watch TV and play computer games.

■ THiNK VALUES ■

Taking care of yourself

1 Which questions in the quiz tell us that these things are important for us?

7	a Being with people
	b Enjoying exercise
	c Sleep
	d Getting rest
	e Giving your brain exercise
	f Being positive
	g Having interests

YOUR SCORE:

Mostly As: You take good care of yourself. You know how to have fun and enjoy life.

Mostly Bs: You take care of yourself OK, but can you do more? Try to find more time for yourself.

Mostly Cs: You don't take good care of yourself. Try to have more fun.

2 **SPEAKING** Compare your ideas with a partner.

Question 7 shows us that being with people is important.

GRAMMAR
Simple present review

1 Complete the sentences with the words in the list. Check your answers in the quiz on page 13.

~~relax~~ | do | does | don't | says

0 I never _relax_ .

1 My best friend _____ I don't smile very often.

2 I _____ really like them.

3 _____ your teacher give you a lot of homework?

4 _____ you like exercise?

2 Look at the sentences in Exercise 1 and the table. Complete the rule with *do*, *does*, *don't*, or *doesn't*.

Affirmative	Negative
I **like** milk.	I **don't like** milk.
You **like** milk.	You **don't like** milk.
He/She/It **likes** milk.	He/She/It **doesn't like** milk.
We **like** milk.	We **don't like** milk.
They **like** milk.	They **don't like** milk.

Questions	Short answers	
Do I **like** milk?	Yes, you **do**.	No, you **don't**.
Do you **like** milk?	Yes, I **do**.	No, I **don't**.
Does he/she/it **like** milk?	Yes, he/she/it **does**.	No, he/she/it **doesn't**.
Do we **like** milk?	Yes, we **do**.	No, we **don't**.
Do they **like** milk?	Yes, they **do**.	No, they **don't**.

RULE: Use the simple present for things that happen regularly or that are always true.

In affirmative sentences:

- with *I*, *you*, *we*, and *they*, use the base form of the verb.
- with *he*, *she*, and *it*, add -*s* (or -*es* with verbs that end -*s*, -*sh*, -*ch*, -*x*, or -*z*).

In negative sentences:

- with *I*, *you*, *we*, and *they*, use [1]_____ .
- with *he*, *she*, and *it*, use [2]_____ .

In questions:

- with *I*, *you*, *we*, and *they*, use the auxiliary [3]_____ .
- with *he*, *she*, and *it*, use the auxiliary [4]_____ .

3 Complete the sentences. Use the simple present of the verbs.

0 I _don't like_ (not like) roller coasters. I _get_ (get) really scared on them.

1 My dad _____ (not sleep) a lot. He only _____ (need) five or six hours.

2 A _____ you _____ (study) English?
   B Yes, I _____ .

3 My dad _____ (cook) really well, but he says he _____ (not enjoy) it.

4 A _____ your sister _____ (play) on the school soccer team?
   B No, she _____ .

5 My grandparents _____ (not like) traveling. They _____ (prefer) to stay at home.

6 My brother _____ (watch) TV all day. He _____ (not do) anything else.

> Workbook page 10

Pronunciation

/s/, /z/, /ɪz/ sounds

Go to page 120.

VOCABULARY
Hobbies

1 Complete the phrases with the words in the list.

~~play~~ | write | have | take | be | collect

0 _play_ an instrument   3 _____ photos

1 _____ in a club   4 _____ a pet

2 _____ a blog   5 _____ things

2 **SPEAKING** Work in pairs. Ask questions about the hobbies in the pictures.

Do you play an instrument?   *What do you play?*

Do you collect something? What ...?

> Workbook page 12

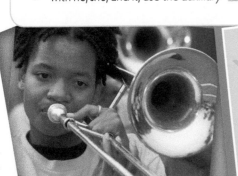

YOUTH CLUB

NAME: **Peter Summers**

ADDRESS: 51 Willow Avenue

PHONE: 550-384-5873

MEMBERSHIP NUMBER: 09173

LISTENING

1 🔊1.20 **Listen to the conversations. Match each one with a picture.**

A

B

C

2 🔊1.20 **Listen again. Complete the sentences with the names in the list.**

~~Tom~~ | Grace | Kayla | Kayla's dad | Jack | Jack's mom

0 _____Tom_____ has a headache.
1 _____ wants to join a baseball team.
2 _____ doesn't have time to relax.
3 _____ thinks music is good for relaxing.
4 _____ wants to be a famous piano player.
5 _____ thinks baseball is for boys.

■ THiNK SELF-ESTEEM ■

Why it's good to have a hobby

1 Circle **the person from Listening Exercise 1.**
I think it's good to have a hobby because …
   1 you can make new friends.
      A Grace   **B** Kayla   **C** Jack
   2 it helps you relax.
      A Grace   **B** Kayla   **C** Jack
   3 you can discover you have new talents.
      A Grace   **B** Kayla   **C** Jack

2 **Copy the diagram into your notebooks and complete it with the hobbies in the list.**

playing the piano | joining a tennis club
collecting stamps | writing a blog
dancing | cooking | watching TV
playing online games | taking photos

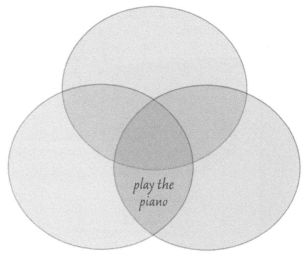

Make friends

play the piano

Relax   *Discover your talents*

3 SPEAKING **Work in pairs. Compare diagrams with your partner.**

> *Playing the piano is good. It helps you to relax.*

4 **What hobbies do you have? Think about why they are good for you. Take notes.**

5 **Tell your partner about your hobbies.**

> *I dance. I'm not very good, but it helps me to relax.*

READING

1 Read the blog and answer the questions.

1 How many people like collecting things?
2 Who has the strangest hobby?

What do you do in your free time?

OK, we know you all like watching TV and playing computer games, but we want to know some of the other things you do when you have some free time. Write us a line or two and let us know.

Posted on January 22

NATHAN
I love taking photos of me with my friends and family. Now I want to get some of me with famous people.

CHLOE
I enjoy lying on my back and looking at clouds. I try to find different shapes in them. It's really relaxing and I occasionally fall asleep doing it.

ISABELLA
Once a week my grandpa takes me out for a milkshake. I love listening to his stories. It's the best.

ADAM
I can't stand walking to school, so I sometimes invent little games to help pass the time. For example, I try to think of an animal or soccer team or city for every letter of the alphabet.

LIZ
I like doing my homework as soon as I get home from school. Is there something wrong with me?

GABRIELA
I really like going for a walk on my own in the forest near our house. There's always something interesting to see, and I never get bored.

LUIZA
I collect bottle caps. They're hard to find these days, so when I go to a restaurant, I always ask if they have drinks in bottles.

DYLAN
I like watching the news on TV. I watch it every day. My friends think I'm weird.

DANIEL
I hate being alone. So when I am by myself I usually start talking to my imaginary friends. But don't tell anyone!

JASMINE
I rarely get bored, but if I do I just go to the library and get a book to learn about something new. It works every time.

MADDIE
I like writing poems. I often write a poem when I don't have anything to do.

2 Read the sentences. Which of the people above do you think is saying each one?

0	A country that starts with R? Easy: Russia.	_Adam_
1	Do you have a book about birds?	
2	Tell me more, please!	
3	Can I take a photo with you?	
4	Sorry, I can't come over now. I want to finish my math homework.	
5	Hey, that one looks just like a cow.	

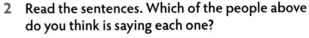

GRAMMAR
like + -ing

1 **Look at the sentences from the blog on page 16. Draw 🙂 or 🙁 next to each one.**

1 I love taking photos. _____

2 I can't stand walking to school. _____

3 I hate being alone. _____

4 I like writing poems. _____

2 **Use the sentences in Exercise 1 to complete the rule.**

> **RULE:** Use the [1] _____ form of the verb after verbs that express likes and dislikes, e.g., *like*, *love*, *hate*, *enjoy*, *can't stand*.
> - To make this form, add [2] _____ to the base verb.
> - If the verb ends in -e, drop the final -e (e.g., *live – living*).
> - If a short verb ends in a consonant + vowel + consonant, we usually double the final consonant before adding the -ing (e.g., *swim – swimming*).

3 **Complete the sentences. Use the *-ing* form of the verbs in the list.**

~~run~~ | visit | swim | eat | ride | talk

0 I hate ____*running*____ to catch the bus to school.

1 My mom and dad enjoy _____ in nice restaurants.

2 My brother can't stand _____ on the telephone.

3 They like _____ in the ocean when it's warm.

4 Donna really likes _____ her horse.

5 We love _____ new places on vacation.

4 **WRITING** **What about you? Write two or three sentences about yourself.**

Adverbs of frequency

5 **Complete the diagram with the words in the list.**

always | occasionally | never | often

6 **Complete the sentences so they are true for you.**

1 I _____ do my homework when I get home.

2 I _____ write thank-you notes for my presents.

3 I am _____ late for school.

4 I _____ watch TV in the mornings.

5 My mom _____ gets angry if I don't clean my room.

6 I _____ turn off the lights when I leave the room.

7 **Complete these sentences from the blog on page 16. Check your answers and complete the rule.**

1 _____ _____ _____ my grandpa takes me out for a milkshake.

2 I watch it (the TV news) _____ _____ .

> **RULE:** Words like *sometimes*, *never*, and *always* come [1]*before / after* the verb be but [2]*before / after* other verbs.
> Phrases like *every day* or *twice a week* can come at the beginning or at the end of a sentence.

8 **Write down things you do …**

every day: ____*give my mom a kiss*____

three times a week: _____

once a year: _____

9 **SPEAKING** **Work in small groups. Compare your answers to Exercises 6 and 8.**

> How often do you go to the movies?

> I usually go once a month.

Workbook page 11 ➤

WRITING
Your routine

Complete the sentences so they are true for you.

1 I rarely _____ weekends.

2 I can't stand _____ .

3 I never _____ when I'm tired.

4 I _____ once a week.

5 I occasionally _____ .

6 I enjoy _____ after school.

Adverbs of frequency

0%				100%
	rarely	sometimes	usually	
1 _____	2 _____		3 _____	4 _____

Olivia's new hobby

1 Look at the photos and answer the questions.

What do you think Olivia's hobby is?
Why does Ryan look worried?

2 🔊 1.21 Now read and listen to the photostory. Check your answers.

LUKE Look. It's Olivia and Megan.
RYAN What are they up to?
LUKE I'm not sure what they're doing, but they're definitely having a good time.
RYAN Let's go and find out.

OLIVIA Hi, Ryan. Hi, Luke.
RYAN Hi, Olivia. So, what are you two doing?
OLIVIA It's my new hobby. I take photos of Megan reading a book in strange places.
LUKE Cool! Can I get a video of you on my phone?
OLIVIA Of course you can. Come on.

LUKE This is great. I think I have a new hobby, too – making videos.
RYAN Be careful, Luke. Don't push too hard.
OLIVIA That's right. Be careful.
MEGAN Don't stop, Luke. I'm having fun.

OLIVIA That's great, Megan.
MEGAN Hurry up. My arms are tired. I need a rest.
OLIVIA Just a few more.
RYAN Look out, Olivia! You're very close to the water.

DEVELOPING SPEAKING

3 Work in pairs. Discuss what happens next in the story. Write down your ideas.

We think Olivia falls in the water.

4 ▶️ EP1 Watch to find out how the story continues.

5 (Circle) the correct word in each sentence.

0 Ryan (tries) / *doesn't try* to warn Olivia.

1 Ryan and Luke *help* / *don't help* her out of the water.

2 Olivia *cries* / *doesn't cry* when she falls into the water.

3 Olivia *laughs* / *doesn't laugh* when she sees her camera.

4 Her camera *is* / *isn't* broken.

5 Luke *tells* / *doesn't tell* them what the surprise is.

6 Luke *gives* / *doesn't give* Olivia the money.

PHRASES FOR FLUENCY

1 Find the expressions 1–5 in the photostory. Who says them? Match them to the definitions a–f.

0 (What are they) up to? _Ryan_ | e

1 Cool! _____ | ☐

2 Come on. _____ | ☐

3 That's right. _____ | ☐

4 Hurry up. _____ | ☐

5 Look out! _____ | ☐

a Be quick.   **d** Let's start.
b I agree.   **e** doing
c Be careful.   **f** Great.

2 Complete the conversation with the expressions in Exercise 1.

SARAH Hi, Nicole. What are you ⁰ ___ *up to* ___ ?

NICOLE Just walking. Are you taking a walk, too?

SARAH ¹ _____ . I'm bored at home.

NICOLE Me, too. We can walk together, if you want.

SARAH ² _____ ! Oh no – ³ _____ ! Mike Smith is coming. I don't like him!

NICOLE ⁴ _____ . Let's walk over here.

SARAH I don't want him to see me. ⁵ _____ !

WordWise
Collocations with *have*

1 Match the sentence parts from the story.

1 ☐ I'm not sure what they're doing,

2 ☐ Don't stop, Luke.

3 ☐ Olivia, I think you *have a problem*.

4 ☐ We're just *having dinner*.

a I'm *having fun*.

b I think your camera's broken.

c It's pizza. Would you like some?

d but they're definitely *having a good time*.

2 Ask and answer the questions in pairs.

1 Who do you have the most fun with?

2 Do you have a good time at school?

3 What do you do when you have a problem?

4 What time do you have dinner?

> Workbook page 12 ➤

FUNCTIONS
Giving warnings and stating prohibition

1 Put the words in order to make sentences.

1 Dan / Be / careful

_____

2 out / Lucy / Look

_____

3 do / that / Don't

_____

4 push / Don't / hard / too

_____

2 Match the sentences in Exercise 1 with the pictures A–D.

A ☐   B ☐   C ☐   D ☐

OBJECTIVES

FUNCTIONS: buying things in a store; talking about what people are doing at the moment

GRAMMAR: present continuous; verbs of perception; simple present vs. present continuous

VOCABULARY: stores; clothes

READING

1 ◀)) 1.22 **Say these prices. Listen and check.**

2 ◀)) 1.23 **What are these objects? Match them with the prices in Exercise 1. Write 1–6 in the boxes. Listen and check.**

3 SPEAKING **Work in pairs. Discuss the following questions. Then compare your ideas with other students.**

Which of the things in Exercise 2 do you …
1 think are cheap?
2 think are expensive?
3 think are important for your life?
4 dream about having?

4 **Look at the picture on page 21. Answer these questions.**

1 Who do you think the boy and girl are?
2 Do you think the girl likes the shirt?

5 ◀)) 1.24 **Read and listen to the script from a soap opera and check your ideas.**

6 **Mark the sentences T (true) or F (false). Correct the false ones in your notebook.**

0 It's six o'clock on Friday afternoon.   *F*
  It's four o'clock on Friday afternoon.
1 Tyler is deciding what to wear.   _____
2 Madison thinks yellow is a good idea. _____
3 Tyler thinks he's good-looking.   _____
4 Tyler wants to buy expensive clothes. _____
5 Tyler wants to be famous.   _____

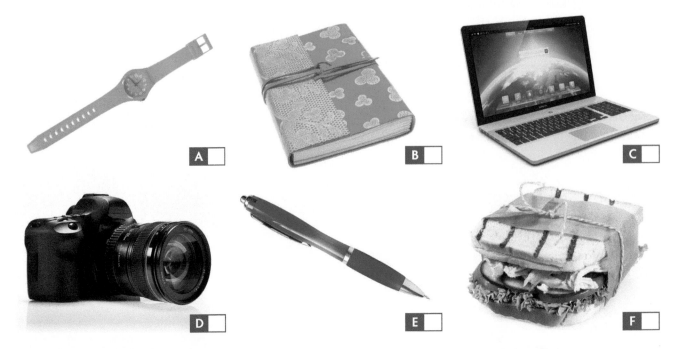

TYLER	Hi, Madison.
MADISON	Where are Mom and Dad?
TYLER	They're out. At the supermarket, I think. They're doing some shopping or something.
MADISON	What are you doing?
TYLER	Me? I'm looking for something.
MADISON	OK. What are you looking for?
TYLER	A shirt. And some pants. I'm going out. It's Friday, and I have plans for tonight. So I'm choosing my clothes.
MADISON	But it's only four o'clock.
TYLER	I know. I need time to choose.
MADISON	Do you need any help? I can help you.
TYLER	No. Well, maybe. OK, yes.
MADISON	Think about colors.
TYLER	I'm thinking. I'm thinking about … yellow.
MADISON	Not a good idea.
TYLER	Why not?
MADISON	Because yellow just isn't interesting.
TYLER	But I like yellow. Like this shirt.
MADISON	I'm trying to help you, Tyler. And I'm telling you – don't wear a yellow shirt.
TYLER	You're laughing. Why are you laughing at me?
MADISON	I'm not laughing at you. I'm laughing at the shirt. It looks terrible.
TYLER	You're right. I need some new ideas.
MADISON	Look at this. Here, in this magazine. See this guy? He's wearing great clothes.
TYLER	Yes, but he's good-looking. And rich, too, probably. I'm not good-looking.
MADISON	Yes, you are! But of course, I'm only saying that because you're my brother. OK, do you have any money?
TYLER	Yes. Why?
MADISON	I want to take you to town – to a clothing store and maybe a shoe store, too.
TYLER	That sounds great. Nothing expensive though.
MADISON	Don't worry. Nice clothes aren't always expensive. Come on.
TYLER	You know, I dream about being famous one day and about having fantastic clothes. Do you dream about that, too?
MADISON	No, I dream about ice cream.
TYLER	That's right, you're only nine years old. OK, we can get ice cream after we buy me some new clothes.

■ THiNK VALUES ■

Fashion and clothes

1   **How important are these for you? Give each one a number from 0 to 5 (0 = not important; 5 = very, very important).**

Clothes – my values:

☐ I want to look cool.
☐ I want to feel comfortable.
☐ I always buy cheap clothes.
☐ I like buying designer clothes.
☐ I love wearing clean clothes.
☐ I like wearing bright colors.
☐ I always buy clothes at the same stores.

2   **SPEAKING** **Work in pairs. Ask and answer questions.**

> How important is it for you to look cool?

> Not very important. I give that 3 points. What about you?

> For me, it's very important – 5 points.

GRAMMAR
Present continuous

1 **Look at the examples of the present continuous. Then complete the rule and the table.**

   1 They**'re doing** some shopping at the supermarket.
   2 He**'s wearing** great clothes.
   3 Why **are** you **laughing** at me?
   4 I**'m not laughing** at you.

> **RULE:** Use the present [1]_____ to talk about things that are happening at or around the time of speaking.
> Form the present continuous with the simple present of [2]_____ + the *-ing* form (e.g., *running* / *doing* / *wearing*, etc.) of the main verb.

Affirmative	Negative
I'm (= I am) working.	I'm not working.
You/We/They ([1]____) working.	You/We/They aren't working.
He/She/It (is) working.	He/She/It [2]_____ working.

Questions	Short answers
[3]_____ I working?	Yes, I am. No, I'm not.
[4]_____ you/we/they working?	Yes, you/we/they [6]_____ . No, you/we/they [7]_____ .
[5]_____ he/she/it working?	Yes, he/she/it [8]_____ . No, he/she/it [9]_____ .

2 **Complete the sentences. Use the present continuous of the verbs.**

   0 Jenny's not here. She's at the mall. She *'s shopping* (shop) for some new sneakers.
   1 They're in the living room. They _____ (play) computer games.
   2 My brother's in the garage. He _____ (clean) his bike.
   3 Steven! You _____ (not listen) to me!
   4 I can't talk now. I _____ (do) my homework.
   5 It's 3–0! We _____ (not play) very well, and we _____ (lose)!
   6 A _____ you _____ (watch) this show?
      B No, I _____ . You can watch a different one if you want.
   7 A What _____ you _____ (do)?
      B I _____ (try) to find some old photos on my computer.

Workbook page 18

VOCABULARY
Stores

1 **Write the names of the stores under the photos.**

newsstand | drugstore | bookstore
clothing store | shoe store | department store
supermarket | sporting goods store

1 _____ 2 _____

3 _____ 4 _____

5 _____ 6 _____

7 _____ 8 _____

2 **SPEAKING Complete the sentences with the names of stores from Exercise 1. Then compare your ideas with other students.**

   1 In my town there's a very good …
      It's called … It's good because …
   2 I often go there because …
   3 I never go into … because they don't interest me.
      I don't often go to … because …

> *In my town there's a very good clothing store.*
> *It's good because the clothes aren't expensive.*

Workbook page 20

GRAMMAR
Verbs of perception

1 **Look at the sentences from the script on page 21. Answer the questions.**

1 *It looks terrible.*   What is "it"?
2 *That sounds great.*   What is "that"?

2 **Match the verbs with the pictures. Then complete the rule.**

1 look   2 sound   3 smell   4 taste

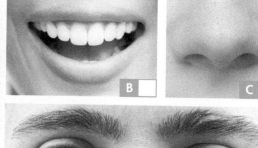
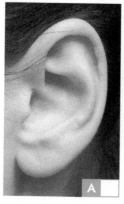

> **RULE:** Verbs of perception are used in the [1]_____ tense when they are used to give an opinion.
>
> The food **tastes** great.   The flowers **smell** nice.
> That idea **sounds** good.   His new shirt **looks** awful!
>
> The words after the verbs of perception are [2]_____ .

3 **Match the responses (a–d) to the first parts of the dialogues (1–4).**

1 I'm going to the movies. ☐
2 My mother's making dinner. ☐
3 I'm wearing my new shoes. ☐
4 Don't you like the juice? ☐

a No. It tastes horrible!   c It smells fantastic.
b That sounds great.   d They look nice.

➡ Workbook page 19

LISTENING

1 🔊 1.25 **Listen. What store is each person in? Write numbers.**

☐ bookstore   ☐ newsstand
☐ clothing store   ☐ sporting goods store

2 🔊 1.25 **Listen again. What does each person want to buy?**

1 _____   3 _____
2 _____   4 _____

FUNCTIONS
Buying things in a store

1 **Read the sentences from the listening. Mark them C (customer) or A (assistant).**

0 Can I help you? *A*
1 Do you have … ? ☐
2 What size are you? ☐
3 Can I try it/them on please? ☐
4 How much is it/are they? ☐
5 That's (twenty dollars), please. ☐
6 Do you have it/them in (blue)? ☐

2 🔊 1.26 **Put the sentences in the correct order 1–9. Listen and check. Practice in pairs.**

☐ A It's $75.
1 A Hello. Can I help you?
☐ A Great. So that's $75, please.
☐ A Sorry, no. Only brown.
☐ A Yes, of course.
☐ B Can I try it on?
☐ B Very nice. I'll take it.
☐ B Yes, please. I like this jacket. Do you have it in black?
☐ B Oh, well, brown's OK. How much is it?

ROLE PLAY Buying clothes in a store

Work in pairs. Student A: Go to page 127. Student B: Go to page 128. Take two or three minutes to prepare. Then have two conversations.

▮ TRAIN TO THiNK ▮
Exploring numbers

1 **You want to buy some new clothes. Here are some things you like. Answer the questions in pairs.**

T-shirt – $8.50   shoes – $24.95   sweater – $19.99
belt – $12   jacket – $35

1 Choose three things. How much do they cost?
2 You have $50.00. Name three things you can buy.
3 You have $100.00. Can you buy all five things?

2 **SPEAKING** **Compare your ideas with a partner.**

> **Pronunciation**
> Contractions
> **Go to page 120.** 🔊

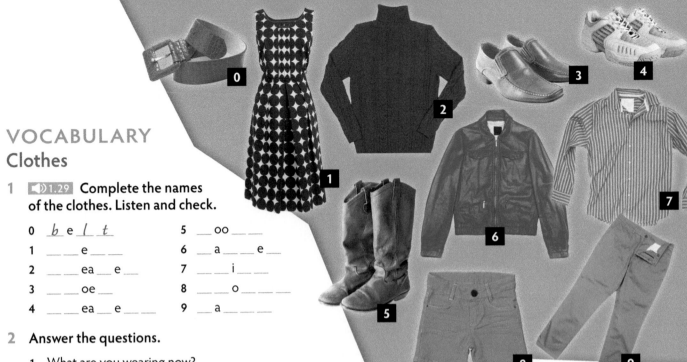

VOCABULARY
Clothes

1 🔊 1.29 **Complete the names of the clothes. Listen and check.**

0	_b_ e _l_ _t_	5	__ oo __ __
1	__ __ e __ __	6	__ a __ __ e __
2	__ __ ea __ e __	7	__ __ i __ __
3	__ __ oe __	8	__ __ __ o __ __ __
4	__ __ ea __ e __ __	9	__ a __ __ __

2 **Answer the questions.**

1 What are you wearing now?
2 What do you usually wear on weekends?
3 What do you never wear?
4 What clothes do you really like / dislike buying?

3 SPEAKING **Work in pairs. Ask and answer the questions in Exercise 2. Then work with another partner.**

> *I'm wearing a green shirt and jeans.*

> *I never wear shorts.*

Workbook page 20

READING

1 **Read the web chat. Answer the questions.**

Who …
1 is interested in the sky? _____
2 is in the kitchen? _____
3 has a problem? _____
4 is in front of a TV? _____
5 is surprising her parents? _____

2 **Think of three things you enjoy that don't need money. Write them down.**

going for a walk   watching TV

_____
_____
_____

3 SPEAKING **Work in pairs. Tell your partner your ideas. Are they things that really don't need money?**

> *I like baking cakes.*

> *But you need money to buy ingredients!*

How not to spend money   ✕

🙂 **JollyMarie**
Saturday, 7:20 p.m.

Wow! Problem. Not a lot of money right now and I don't want to spend it. I'm tired of spending money! So here I am at home and I'm thinking – what can I do that's free? (and fun lol)

👍 👎   LIKE • COMMENT • SHARE

EllieParsons
just now

Oh JollyMarie, it's not such a big deal. My friends and I often have a picnic on Sundays, and I make the sandwiches the night before. So right now, it's Saturday night, and I'm making sandwiches. hehehe

PeteJ
47 minutes ago

I really like going to the movies, but it can be expensive – especially because my friends and I often go out for pizza after the movie. So tonight I'm watching a movie on TV. I'm really enjoying it. And it's free! It's incredible how many movies there are on TV these days.

RonnieRaver
42 minutes ago

It's funny, PeteJ – I'm just like you (going to the movies, I mean). Right now, I'm not watching a movie – I'm watching the stars! It's fantastic. I'm having a really good time here!

goodgirl
1 hour ago

I always go into town on the weekend – and I usually spend money! It's very easy to buy things if you go to a shopping mall. So this weekend I'm staying home. Right now I'm just reading a book – my parents can't believe it! lol

GRAMMAR
Simple present vs. present continuous

1 Look at the examples. Complete the rule.

simple present

I usually **watch** movies at the theater.

I **make** the sandwiches the night before.

I always **go** into town.

present continuous

Right now, I**'m watching** a movie on TV.

It's Saturday night, and I**'m making** sandwiches.

This weekend, I**'m staying** at home.

> **RULE:** Use the ¹_____ to talk about habits, routines, and things that are generally or always true.
> Use the ²_____ to talk about temporary things that are happening around the moment of speaking.

2 Match the sentences with the pictures. Write 1–4 in the boxes.

1 She sings well.

2 She's singing well.

3 He plays soccer.

4 He's playing soccer.

A

B

C

D

> **LOOK!** These verbs are almost never used in the present continuous:
>
> believe | know | understand | mean
> remember | need | like | hate | want
>
> *I **know** the answer.* (Not: ~~I'm knowing the answer.~~)
> *I **understand** the problem.* (Not: ~~I am understanding the problem.~~)

3 (Circle) the correct options.

1 We *always wear* / *'re always wearing* a uniform to school.

2 Paula *wears* / *is wearing* black jeans today.

3 Come inside! It *rains* / *'s raining*.

4 It *rains* / *'s raining* a lot in February.

5 Dad *cooks* / *'s cooking* at the moment.

6 My mother *cooks* / *'s cooking* lunch every Sunday.

7 Steve's terrible! He *never listens* / *'s never listening* to the teacher!

8 Can you be quiet, please? I *listen* / *'m listening* to the music.

4 Complete the sentences. Use the simple present or present continuous form of the verbs.

0 Mandy usually __goes__ (go) to school on her bike, but today she __is walking__ (walk).

1 We _____ (have) science class on Mondays. Today we _____ (learn) about trees.

2 Tom _____ (go) shopping today. He _____ (want) to buy a new camera.

3 I _____ (know) her face, but I _____ (not remember) her name.

4 Alex _____ (not watch) the game because he _____ (not like) soccer very much.

5 What _____ this word _____ (mean)? I _____ (not understand) it.

Workbook page 19

SPEAKING

1 Look at these photos. Who are the people in each one?

2 Work in pairs. Discuss the questions.

For each person, say …

• who they are.

• what they do.

• what they are doing.

> *It's Beyoncé. She's a …*
> *She's …*

Culture

1 Look at the photos. Name one or two things you can buy in each market.

- Where can you see stalls?
- Where can you see a canal?

2 🔊 1.30 Read and listen to the article. Match the photos with the places. Write the numbers 1–5 in the boxes.

A

World markets

Wherever you go in the world, you find malls and stores – but you can find wonderful markets in most cities, too. Here's a selection from five different countries.

1 The **Spice Bazaar** in **Istanbul** is popular with both tourists and people from Istanbul. There are lots of stalls, and they all sell many different kinds of spices, sweets, and nuts. You can buy spices from a lot of countries (like Iran, China, Russia, and of course Turkey), and the smells and colors are amazing.

2 **Khlong Lat Phli** is a very unusual market about 80 kilometers south of **Bangkok**, Thailand. Early every morning, hundreds of local people sell fruit and vegetables from their boats on the canals. It's not the only boat market in the country, but it's a very popular tourist one.

3 Do you like fish? Then the **Tsukiji Market** in **Tokyo** is the right place for you. It is the biggest seafood market in the world, and it never closes! It's very busy between the hours of 4:00 and 5:00 a.m., when people from the restaurants in Tokyo buy the fresh fish that they need for the day. It is also very popular with tourists, but they can only visit the market later in the day, after the early morning buying and selling.

B

4 In **Madrid** there is a famous open-air market called **El Rastro**, which is open on Sunday mornings. There are more than 1,000 stalls that sell many different things: books, CDs, paintings, antiques – beautiful old things. One of the streets sells only animals and birds. And of course, visitors can get something to eat and drink. There are many street musicians with their guitars making music, too.

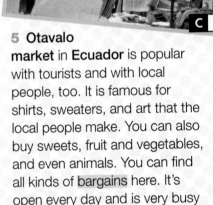
C

5 **Otavalo market** in **Ecuador** is popular with tourists and with local people, too. It is famous for shirts, sweaters, and art that the local people make. You can also buy sweets, fruit and vegetables, and even animals. You can find all kinds of bargains here. It's open every day and is very busy on Saturdays.

D

E

3 VOCABULARY **There are eight highlighted words in the article. Match the words with these meanings. Write the words.**

0 tables or small stores in a market — *stalls*
1 not inside a building _____
2 things to eat from the sea _____
3 different or surprising _____
4 small man-made rivers _____
5 full of people _____
6 liked by a lot of people _____
7 things that you buy at a low price _____

4 **Read the article again. Correct the information in these sentences in your notebook.**

0 All the spices at the Istanbul Spice Bazaar are from Turkey.
Not all the spices are from Turkey. You can buy spices from a lot of countries.

1 At Khlong Lat Phli, people sell spices from their boats.
2 The Tsukiji Market closes between four and five in the morning.
3 Tourists can go to the Tsukiji Market in the early morning.
4 You can't get food at El Rastro.
5 You can buy clothes from around the world at Otavalo market.

SPEAKING

1 **Make sentences about the markets that are true for you. Use adjectives from the list or other adjectives if you want.**

fantastic | interesting | fascinating
exciting | unusual | attractive

I think the ... market is fantastic / isn't very interesting because ...

2 **Work in groups. Compare your sentences and ideas.**

> *I think the Istanbul Spice Bazaar is fantastic because ...*

WRITING
An email to say what you're doing

1 **Read the email from Paul to his friend Lucy. Answer the questions.**

1 Where is Paul and what is he doing?
2 Where are his father and sister?
3 What is Paul's family watching tonight?

2 **How does Paul start his email? And how does he finish it? Complete the table with the words in the list.**

Dear | Love | Hello | See you soon | Best wishes

starting an email	ending an email
Hi (Lucy),	Hope you are OK.
1 _____ (Mike)	Bye
2 _____ (Mr. Jones)	3 _____
	4 _____
	5 _____

3 **Look at paragraphs 1 and 2 of Paul's email. Match the functions with the paragraphs. Write a–d.**

Paragraph 1: _____ and _____ .
Paragraph 2: _____ and _____ .

a saying what you are doing
b talking about your plans
c saying where you are
d a description of the place where you are

4 **Check (✓) the things Paul writes about in his email.**

1 what he likes about the city ☐
2 when he is coming home ☐
3 his plans for tonight ☐
4 where he is staying ☐
5 what his mother/father/sister are doing ☐
6 how Lucy is ☐

5 **Write an email to a friend (100–120 words). Imagine you are in a café or store in a shopping mall. Use the example email and language above to help you.**

To: Lucy10@email.com
Subject: Hello from Madrid!

Hi Lucy! How are things with you?
(1) I'm in Madrid right now – we're here on vacation. Madrid is a really cool place. There are stores, markets, and of course the soccer stadium! We're staying in a small hotel in the middle of Madrid, and it's really nice.
(2) I'm sitting in a café right now with my mom, and we're having a soda because it's really hot today! My father and sister are at a market near here. They're looking for some shoes for my sister. Tonight we're going to a flamenco dancing show. I don't especially like dancing, but all the family does, so … !
(3) OK, my father and sister are coming back, so I'm going now. Write soon and tell me how you are.
Hope you're OK.
Paul

CAMBRIDGE ENGLISH: Key

THiNK EXAMS

READING AND WRITING
Part 3: Multiple-choice replies

Workbook page 17

1 Complete the five conversations. Choose the correct answer A, B, or C.

0 What are you doing?
- **A** I play computer games.
- **B** I'm a doctor.
- **C** I'm trying to find my school bag. *(circled)*

1 How often are you late for school?
- **A** on Mondays
- **B** about once a month
- **C** at ten o'clock

2 Does your brother go to your school?
- **A** Yes, he does go.
- **B** Yes, he goes.
- **C** Yes, he does.

3 What do you think of my new haircut?
- **A** It looks really good.
- **B** It's looking really good.
- **C** It sounds great.

4 Do you like doing puzzles?
- **A** Yes, I like.
- **B** Three times a week.
- **C** No, I can't stand them.

5 Do you live in a big town?
- **A** No, we aren't.
- **B** Yes, we do.
- **C** No, you don't.

Part 6: Word completion

Workbook page 43

2 Read the descriptions of clothes. What is the word for each one? The first letter is already there. There is one space for each other letter in the word.

0 You can wear this over your shirt when you go out.
j a c k e t

1 Wear these shoes to play sports. s _ _ _ _ _ _ _ _ _

2 Put this on if it's cold. s _ _ _ _ _ _ _

3 Some boys wear pants to school, other boys wear these. s _ _ _ _ _

4 You wear this around the top of your pants.
b _ _ _ _

5 A lot of teenagers wear these. j _ _ _ _ _

LISTENING
Part 1: Multiple-choice pictures

Workbook page 25

3 🔊 1.31 You will hear five short conversations. There is one question for each conversation. For each question, choose the right answer (A, B, or C).

0 What are the girls talking about?

A ☐ B ✓ C ☐

1 When does Oliver play tennis?

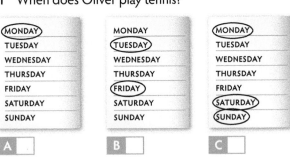

A ☐ B ☐ C ☐

2 Where is Brian?

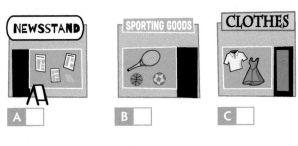

A ☐ B ☐ C ☐

3 What is Molly's hobby?

A ☐ B ☐ C ☐

4 How much is the red sweater?

A ☐ B ☐ C ☐

TEST YOURSELF

VOCABULARY

1 **Complete the sentences with the words in the list. There are two extra words.**

newsstand | take | dress | club | write | plays | collects
sporting goods store | supermarket | sweater | shoe store | belt

1   I want to _____ a blog about pop music.
2   If you're cold, why don't you put on a _____ ?
3   She _____ the guitar and the piano. She's really good at both.
4   I need to go to the _____ and buy some tennis balls.
5   My dad _____ old toy cars. He's just a big child!
6   You need some new boots. Let's go to the _____ .
7   I'm thinking about joining the French _____ , but I don't have a lot of time.
8   Your pants are falling down. You need a _____ .
9   Can you get some eggs and some milk when you go to the _____ , please?
10 I always _____ a lot of photos when I travel.

/10

GRAMMAR

2 **Complete the sentences with the words in the list.**

's working | 're writing | works | plays | 're playing | write

1   My dad's a cook. He _____ at a restaurant in town.
2   I like poetry. I _____ at least five poems every week.
3   Mom's in her office. She _____ on something very important.
4   Paul's in a band. He _____ the drums.
5   Ethan and Dan are on the computer. They _____ their blog.
6   Lucy and Rachel are in the yard. They _____ soccer.

3 **Find and correct the mistake in each sentence.**

1   I can't stand to eat carrots.   _____
2   We don't playing very well today.   _____
3   They doesn't like playing video games.   _____
4   That sandwich is tasting very good.   _____
5   Does you speak French?   _____
6   He goes always swimming on weekends.   _____

/12

FUNCTIONAL LANGUAGE

4 **Write the missing words.**

1   A   Be _____ ! It looks very dangerous.
    B   Don't worry. I'm _____ fun.
2   A   How _____ do you watch TV?
    B   _____ day when I get home from school.
3   A   Look _____ ! There's a dog coming.
    B   And it _____ look happy. Let's run!
4   A   Please _____ shout! The baby is asleep.
    B   Oh, OK. I'm _____ .

/8

MY SCORE   /30

| 22 – 30 |
| 10 – 21 |
| 0 – 9 |

3 FOOD FOR LIFE

READING

1 What food and drink in the picture can you name? What food and drink do you know in English?

2 Make sentences that are true for you. Compare your ideas in class.

I	always often sometimes never	have … for	breakfast. lunch. dinner.

3 Look at the photos on page 31. Ask your teacher for the words you don't know. Then answer the questions.

> What's … in English?

Can you think of a food that …

- comes from another country?
- has a lot of vitamins?
- is very healthy?
- is unusual?
- is good for your hair and skin?

4 ◀)) 1.32 **Read and listen to the article. Match the parts of the sentences.**

0	In Japan people think square watermelons	*e*
1	Bananas are popular because they	
2	In Iceland people don't like	
3	Honey is healthy and good	
4	Avocado is a dessert in	
5	Potato clocks are very popular in	
6	Sugar is not only in sweets. It's also in	

a normal ice cream.
b Brazil.
c for our looks.
d West Africa.

e make very special presents.
f fruit.
g help us feel good.

5 SPEAKING **Work in pairs. Two of the "food facts" in Exercise 4 are not true. Which ones do you think they are?**

> I don't think that people give square watermelons as special presents in Japan.

> I think it's true that …

> Yes, I think so, too. / No, I think that's impossible.

> What do you think about statement number …?

> I'm not sure. I think … Do you agree?

> Yes, I do. / No, I don't. I think …

Food facts or food fiction?

In Japan, square watermelons are very popular. People often buy them as presents. They are very special, but of course very expensive, too. Round watermelons do not cost as much.

People all over the world love bananas. Food experts say that bananas contain a chemical that helps the body to produce serotonin. It's sometimes called the body's own "happiness hormone."

People in Iceland love eating unusual flavors of ice cream. There is pizza ice cream, sausage ice cream, and even fish ice cream, and they are all very popular. People eat them with a lot of ketchup. But you don't find any lemon or mango ice cream there. Icelanders just don't like those flavors.

Honey is very healthy. It has lots of vitamins. Some people say that honey makes us beautiful. They think it's good for the hair and the skin. Honey is also very special because it is the only food we eat that never goes bad. We can eat 4,000-year-old honey!

The avocado is a fruit, not a vegetable. It comes from Central and South America originally, but now it grows in hot places all over the world. Many people like avocados as an appetizer before their main meal. But how many people eat it as a dessert? Well, in Brazil, people eat avocados with ice cream and milk.

People in West Africa use a potato clock to tell time. Every morning, they put exactly 7.5 kilos of potatoes in the clock. It looks like a big pot. They put it on the fire. They know that it takes two hours to cook the potatoes.

Everybody knows that fruit has sugar in it. But how much sugar is there in a lemon? A lot. More than there is in a strawberry!

■ THiNK VALUES ■

Food and health

1 Complete the five conversations. Choose the correct answer A, B, or C.

1 Do you want some ice cream?
   A No, thanks. Can I have an apple or a banana?
   B She's not hungry.
   C They're very good.

2 Have some water.
   A I drink it.
   B No, thanks, I'm not thirsty.
   C Look at them.

3 Would you like more chocolate?
   A It's over there.
   B Yes, I do.
   C I'd love some, but I'm trying not to eat too much.

4 Do you eat any vegetables?
   A I hate apples.
   B It's fast food.
   C No, I don't. I don't like them.

5 Have some cookies.
   A Thanks, I'll have just one.
   B You can have a banana.
   C I'm very healthy.

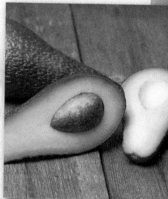

2 SPEAKING Work in pairs. Compare your answers. Do the people care about healthy food?

The person in number 1	doesn't want a … likes … never eats / drinks …	He/She asks for … He/She says … He/She wants …

I think he/she	cares about … doesn't care about …

VOCABULARY
Food and drink

1 🔊 1.33 **Write the names of the food under the pictures. Listen and check.**

green beans | omelette | carrots | peppers | cake | coffee | yogurt | salad | chili | tacos

1 _____

2 _____

3 _____

4 _____

5 _____

6 _____

7 _____

8 _____

9 _____

10 _____

2 **SPEAKING** Work in pairs. Ask and answer questions to find out three things your partner likes and doesn't like.

Workbook page 30

GRAMMAR
Count and noncount nouns

1 **Read the sentences. Then (circle) the correct words in the rule.**

1 Can I have a carrot?
2 I don't like rice.
3 I don't like peppers.

> **RULE:** Nouns that you can count (*one carrot, two carrots*, etc.) are ¹count / noncount nouns.
> Nouns you cannot count are ²count / noncount nouns. They have no plural form.

2 **Look at the photos at the top of the page. Which are count nouns? Which are noncount nouns?**

a/an, some, any

3 **Complete the sentences with *a/an*, *some*, and *any*. Then (circle) the correct words in the rule.**

1 A Would you like _____ water?
  B No, thanks. I have _____ coffee.
2 Can I have _____ apple or _____ banana?
3 Have _____ cookies.
4 Are there _____ vegetables in the kitchen?
5 There isn't _____ milk in the fridge.

> **RULE:** Use *a/an* with ¹singular / plural count nouns.
> Use *some* with ²singular / plural count and with noncount nouns.
> Use *any* in questions and in ³affirmative / negative sentences.
> Use *some* in questions when offering or requesting something.

4 **Complete the sentences with *a/an*, *some*, and *any*.**

1 A Would you like _____ vegetables?
  B Yes, I'd like _____ carrots, please.
2 A I'd like _____ strawberries, please.
  B Sorry, we don't have _____ .
3 I'd like _____ tomatoes.
4 I don't want _____ coffee.
5 Can I have _____ orange, please?
6 Do you want _____ sugar in your tea?

(how) much / (how) many / a lot of / lots of

5 **Look at the examples. Complete the rule.**

How much sugar is there in a lemon?	How many people eat avocado as a dessert?
I don't eat **much** chocolate.	We don't have **many** apples.
Bananas have **a lot of** sugar.	**A lot of** people like avocados.
Watermelons have **lots of** water.	Honey has **lots of** vitamins.

> **RULE:** We typically use *(How) much* and *(How) many* in questions and negative sentences.
> Use *many* with plural ¹_____ nouns and *much* with ²_____ nouns.
> Use *a lot of / lots of* with both count and noncount ³_____ .

6 (Circle) the correct words in questions 1–6. Then match them with the answers a–f.

1 ☐ How *much / many* apples do you want?
2 ☐ How *much / many* sugar is there in an avocado?
3 ☐ Are there *much / many* boys in your class?
4 ☐ How *much / many* peppers are there?
5 ☐ How *much / many* time do you have?
6 ☐ Do you have *many / a lot of* homework?

a I think there are about five.
b Just one, please.
c Only ten minutes.
d No, I don't have any.
e I have no idea. I don't think it's a lot.
f Yes, there are 12, and 5 girls.

Workbook page 28

LISTENING

1 🔊 **1.34** Complete the menu with words from the list. Listen and check.

cheesecake | fries | tomato | onion rings | chicken
spinach and mushroom | hot chocolate | fruit

BLUES CAFÉ MENU

APPETIZERS
green salad
¹_____ soup
mushroom soup

LUNCH SPECIALS
²_____ omelette
cheese omelette
steak
grilled ³_____
pasta with tomatoes

SIDE DISHES
⁴_____
⁵_____

DESSERTS
yogurt and strawberries
vanilla and
chocolate ice cream
⁶_____

DRINKS
⁷_____ juice
⁸_____
tea
coffee
mineral water

2 🔊 **1.35** Jane and Sam are in the Blues Café. Listen and find out who eats more. Listen again and complete the sentences below.

1 Jane wants the ...
2 Sam orders ...
3 Sam is still ...

3 🔊 **1.35** Complete the sentences with *get, menu, drink, we'd, some,* and *check*. Then listen again and check.

Waiter:	Customer:
Welcome to the Blues Cafe. →	Hello. ¹_____ like something to eat.
Here's the ²_____ . →	Thanks.
What would you like to ³_____ ? →	Some orange juice for me, please.
I'll be right back. ←	And for me, just ⁴_____ water, please.
All right! What can I ⁵_____ you? →	I'd like the cheese omelette.
Would you like … ? →	No, thanks. Just the omelette.
Of course. That's $28, please. ←	Can we have the ⁶_____ , please?
And here's your change. Thanks very much. ←	Here you are.

4 SPEAKING Work in groups. One is the waiter, the others are customers. Order meals. Use the menu in Exercise 1 and the conversations in Exercise 3.

▇ THiNK SELF-ESTEEM ▇

Being happy

1 Read these statements. Check (✓) the ones that you think are important for being happy.

1 There's no "right" body size. Happy people come in all shapes and sizes. ☐
2 You can only find out what kind of person someone is if you get to know them better. ☐
3 Never laugh about people for being too thin, too short, too tall, or too fat. ☐
4 Never laugh at other people's jokes about people's looks. That's unfair and it hurts. ☐
5 Being thin is not the same as being healthy and happy. ☐
6 Like yourself for who you are and for the things you are good at. ☐

2 SPEAKING Work in pairs. Say what you think is important for being happy.

Pronunciation
Vowel sounds: /ɪ/ and /i/
Go to page 120. 🔊

READING

1 Look at Jenny's blog for not more than 15 seconds and answer the questions. Then read and check your answers.

1 How old is Jenny? _____
2 How is she feeling? _____
3 What's the problem? _____

2 Read the blog again. Answer the questions in your notebook.

1 How do Jenny's parents react to Jeremy's cooking?
2 What does Jeremy sometimes do with the food his family doesn't eat?
3 Why does Jeremy sing when he serves his spaghetti?
4 Why does Jenny say that her mom and dad's dance class is "unhealthy"?

WRITING
Your favorite meal

1 Put the sentences or phrases in order to make an email from Jenny to her friend.

a ☐ Actually, this week it's not a surprise.
b ☐ My brother always cooks a surprise meal for us then.
c ☐ Best, Jenny
d ☐ Would you like to come and try this week's surprise?
e ☐ Are you free on Friday night?
f ☐ He's making omelettes with beans and strawberries.
g ☐ And for dessert it's some ice cream and strawberries.
h ☐ 1 Dear Jimmy,
i ☐ Doesn't that sound good?

2 Write out the email in your notebook.

3 Write an email describing your favorite or least favorite meal.

Thirteenandsosmart.com

HOME   ABOUT   NEWS   CONTACT

MY BLOG ABOUT MY DAY AND
OTHER IMPORTANT THINGS

FRIDAY, MARCH 17

Not a good day. My older brother Jeremy is cooking tonight. "What's the problem?" I can hear you saying. Well, the problem is that you don't know my brother. You don't know how he cooks. And you don't know that every Friday is a nightmare for me because my parents go to their dance class. When they come back, we all sit down, and Jeremy starts serving what he calls "another surprise meal." Jeremy isn't a bad cook. He's a catastrophe!

First of all, he always cooks too many things, like fish, steak, chili, roast chicken, and sausages. All on one plate! That's too much food for a week! How can one person eat all that in one meal? Mom and Dad don't say a word, of course. They're too polite. And they don't want to quit their dance classes.

Spaghetti tonight. When Jeremy says "spaghetti," he doesn't say it. He sings it (he loves cooking spaghetti – well, he loves cooking anything!). But that doesn't make a difference. It tastes terrible. There isn't enough tomato sauce on it. There's too much pasta. And there's too much salt. Yuck! Another one of my brother's favorites is vegetable soup. It's always too spicy, and there are never enough vegetables in it. And he puts in little pieces of fish, steak, chicken, and sausages. You can guess where they're from. It's the leftovers from the week before.

My brother's desserts aren't bad. He gets them at the supermarket. Dessert is usually ice cream with strawberries or chocolate mousse with pieces of mango. But of course, there are never enough strawberries, and there's never enough ice cream. I want to talk to Mom and Dad today. I want them to quit dancing. It's not healthy. You know what I mean. It's unhealthy for me when they go dancing every Friday!

GRAMMAR

too many / too much / (not) enough + noun

1 **Complete the sentences with *much*, *many*, or *enough* and then complete the rule.**

1 He always cooks **too** _____ **things**.

2 There's **too** _____ **salt** in the spaghetti.

3 There isn't _____ **tomato sauce** on it.

4 There aren't _____ **vegetables** in the soup.

5 There isn't _____ **sugar** in my coffee.

> **RULE:** Use *too* [1]_____ with count nouns and *too* [2]_____ with noncount nouns.
> Use (not) *enough* with [3]_____ and [4]_____ nouns.

2 **Complete the sentences with *too much*, *too many*, or *not enough*.**

1 There are _____ mushrooms on this pizza. I hate them.

2 There's _____ salt in this soup. I can't eat it.

3 There is _____ sugar in my coffee. Can I have some more, please?

4 There are _____ chairs. Can you stand?

5 There are _____ cars on the road. It's dangerous to ride my bike.

6 We have _____ homework tonight. I want to watch TV.

too + adjective, (not +) adjective + enough

3 **Use the example sentences to ⓒircle the correct options in the rule.**

*His vegetable soup is always **too spicy**.*
*This pizza **isn't hot enough**.*

> **RULE:** We use *too* + adjective to say that something is [1]*more / less* than we like or want.
> We use *not* + adjective + *enough* to say that something is [2]*more / less* than we like or want.

4 **Complete the sentences.**

0 The test is too easy. *It isn't hard enough.*

1 The movie isn't exciting enough. _____.

2 The T-shirt is too expensive. _____.

3 It's not warm enough today. _____.

4 Your bike's too small for me. _____.

5 His car's not fast enough. _____.

5 **Complete with *not enough* or *too*.**

I like my country, but there's [1]_____ much rain here in the summer, and it's usually [2]_____ warm _____ to swim. It's [3]_____ boring here in the summer. That's why we always go to Mexico for vacation. There are miles of beaches, so there are never [4]_____ many tourists. And I love the food – which is why I often eat [5]_____ much!

> Workbook page 29

VOCABULARY

Adjectives to talk about food

1 **Write the adjectives under the photos.**

roasted | boiled | grilled | fried

2 **Number the words from 1 (very good) to 4 (very bad).**

nice ___ horrible ___ delicious ___ boring ___

3 **SPEAKING** **Work in pairs. Ask and answer questions. Use the words from Exercise 2.**

boiled or roasted vegetables? | grilled or fried chicken?
grilled or roasted steak? | boiled or fried eggs?
grilled or fried fish?

> *What do you prefer, grilled or fried chicken?*

> *Fried chicken. It's delicious.*

4 **How do you say these words in your language? Write two types of food next to each word.**

sweet | spicy | fresh | tasty
yummy | fatty | disgusting | salty

sweet: chocolate, strawberries

> Workbook page 30

The picnic

1 🔊 1.38 **Read and listen to the photostory and answer the questions.**

What food and drink do Megan and Luke have?

Why is Olivia unhappy?

MEGAN A picnic. I love picnics. What a great idea, Ryan.

OLIVIA Yes, Ryan. It was an awesome idea.

RYAN Don't be so surprised. It's not my first one.

LUKE Umm. Actually, I think it probably is.

OLIVIA What drinks do you have, Megan?

MEGAN Let me see. I have orange juice, lemonade, and apple juice. Oh, and some water as well.

OLIVIA That's great. What about you, Ryan?

RYAN I have lots of fruit: apples and bananas. Oh, and a couple of chocolate bars.

OLIVIA Luke? What about the sandwiches?

LUKE Well, I have chicken salad, tuna, and a steak sandwich, too.

OLIVIA That's all? But what about me? I can't eat that.

LUKE Why not?

OLIVIA Because I have a problem with eating meat. I'm a vegetarian, remember?

LUKE So what? You can have the tuna sandwich, then.

RYAN Oh, Luke! Olivia is really upset now.

LUKE Is she upset with me? Why? Tell me. I have no idea.

MEGAN She's a vegetarian, Luke. She doesn't eat meat. It's important to her.

LUKE Don't vegetarians eat fish?

MEGAN Maybe some do, but not Olivia.

LUKE Oh, no!

DEVELOPING SPEAKING

2 Work in pairs. Discuss what happens next in the story. Write down your ideas.

We think Olivia eats a tuna sandwich.

3 ◻◀ **EP2** Watch to find out how the story continues.

4 Mark the sentences T (True) or F (False).

1 Luke feels bad for not thinking about Olivia. _____
2 Ryan has lots of cookies. _____
3 Megan and Ryan play soccer against the other two. _____
4 Luke secretly makes a phone call. _____
5 They don't enjoy the soccer game. _____
6 Luke buys Olivia a pizza with no meat. _____

PHRASES FOR FLUENCY

1 Find the expressions 1–5 in the story. Who says them? Match them to the definitions.

0	Actually, …	*Luke*	e
1	… as well.	_____	☐
2	… a couple of …	_____	☐
3	What about (me)?	_____	☐
4	So what?	_____	☐
5	upset with …	_____	☐

a too
b unhappy with
c one or two (but not many)
d What is the situation (for me)?
e In fact, …
f Why is that a problem?

2 Complete the conversations. Use the expressions in Exercise 1.

1 A Mom, John has his lunch, but _____ me?
  B Well, I'm making _____ cheese and tomato sandwiches for you right now.
  A Cool! Can I have an apple _____ ?

2 A I broke your watch. I'm sorry. Are you _____ me?
  B It's OK. _____ , it wasn't a very good watch.

3 A I can't go to the movies. I have homework.
  B _____ ? You can do it this weekend.

WordWise
Expressions with *have*

1 Complete the things that Luke and Olivia say.

1 I have a _____ with eating meat.
2 I have _____ idea.
3 You go on. I have _____ to do first.

2 Complete the sentences with the expressions in the list.

a problem | an idea | a headache |
time | something to do

0 A Dad! I have ___*a problem*___ with my English homework.
  B English? Sorry! I can't help you.
1 A Are you OK? Is something wrong?
  B I have _____ . I want to go to bed.
2 A What can we do this afternoon?
  B I don't know.
  C Oh, I have _____ !
3 A Nina, can you help me, please?
  B I'm sorry, Tom. Class starts in two minutes! I don't have _____ .
4 A Let's go to town tomorrow.
  B Sorry, no, I have _____ tomorrow. It's a secret!

Workbook page 30 ➔

FUNCTIONS
Apologizing

1 Who says these sentences? Mark them O (Olivia) or L (Luke).

1 I'm really sorry. ___
2 I feel bad. ___
3 Don't worry. ___
4 It's OK. ___

2 ◀)) **1.39** Complete the conversation. Listen and check. Then act it out in pairs.

MAN   Oh, no. I'm really [1] _____ .
WOMAN [2] _____ worry. It's not my favorite picture.
MAN   But it's broken. I [3] _____ really bad.
WOMAN [4] _____ OK. I don't really like it anyway.

3 Work in pairs. Write a short dialogue for the picture below. Act it out.

4 FAMILY TIES

OBJECTIVES

FUNCTIONS: talking about families; asking for permission

GRAMMAR: possessive adjectives and pronouns; *whose* and possessive *'s*; *was / were*

VOCABULARY: family members; feelings

READING

1 Find the pairs of words.

> daughter   brother   father
> wife   husband   mother
> son   sister

2 SPEAKING Describe each person in the picture. Use two words from Exercise 1.

> *The girl is a daughter and a sister.*

3 Work in pairs. Write down as many examples as you can of the following.

1 a TV brother and sister _____

_____

2 a TV husband and wife _____

_____

4 SPEAKING Compare your ideas with another pair.

5 ◀))1.40 Read and listen to the article on page 39. Do they mention any of the TV families you talked about?

6 Read the article again. Correct the information in these sentences.

1 Bart Simpson has a cat named Santa's Little Helper.

_____

2 Lisa Simpson has one aunt.

_____

3 Ben Tennyson is on vacation in Europe.

_____

4 Ben can change into 12 different aliens.

_____

5 Greg Heffley has a little brother named Roderick.

_____

6 Greg's ideas are always successful.

_____

TV families

Who are your favorite TV families? It's not easy. There are so many great ones to choose from. But to help you start thinking, here are some of ours.

Everyone knows *The Simpsons* – Bart, his mom and dad Marge and Homer, his sisters Lisa and Maggie. And then there's Grandpa and those horrible aunts, Patty and Selma. And let's not forget Bart's dog, Santa's Little Helper. I love watching this family and their adventures around the town of Springfield. They get into all kinds of trouble, but they never forget they are a family. And they always make me laugh. I love this show. Thanks, Dad, for introducing me to it.

When I was eight, *Ben 10* was my favorite TV program. The story is crazy. Ten-year-old Ben Tennyson is spending his summer vacation with his grandpa and his cousin Gwen. They are driving around the U.S. One day Ben finds a strange watch and puts it on. Suddenly, he is an alien. With this watch he can turn into ten different space creatures. But he needs these powers because an evil alien wants Ben's new watch. So Ben spends the rest of the vacation fighting lots of monsters from outer space. But of course, he still has time to fight with his cousin, too.

The Heffley family are the stars of *Diary of a Wimpy Kid*, a really popular series of books and movies centered around Greg, the middle son of the family. Greg lives with his mom and dad, his little brother Manny, and his big brother Roderick. He's just a "normal" kid who writes about his life in a journal. OK, so the Heffley family is not really a TV family, but they show the movies on TV a lot, so we think we can choose them. We want the Heffleys on our list because they are so funny. And we really love Greg and all the problems he has with his great ideas that never work out.

So these are three of our favorite TV families. Now write in and tell us about some of yours.

■ THiNK VALUES ■

TV families

1 **Think about your favorite TV family. Check (✓) the things they do.**

My favorite TV family is _____ .

- They help each other.
- They fight a lot.
- They laugh a lot.
- They spend a lot of time together.
- They talk about their problems.
- They are good friends.

2 **SPEAKING** **Work in pairs. Tell your partner about your favorite TV family. Are they a good family?**

> *The Simpsons are usually a good family because ...*

> *But sometimes they ...*

GRAMMAR
Possessive adjectives and pronouns

1 **Complete the sentences with the words in the list. Look at the article on page 39 and check your answers.**

our | ours | your | yours

1 Who are _____ favorite TV families?
2 Here are some of _____ .
3 These are three of _____ favorite TV families.
4 Write in and tell us about some of _____ .

2 **Complete the rule with *pronouns* and *adjectives*. Then complete the table.**

> **RULE:** Possessive [1]_____ come before a noun to show who something belongs to: *It's **my** book.*
> Possessive [2]_____ can take the place of the possessive adjective and the noun: *The book is **mine**.*

possessive adjectives	possessive pronouns
0 It's __my__ book.	The book is __mine__
1 It's your book.	The book is _____ .
2 It's _____ book.	The book is hers.
3 It's _____ book.	The book is his.
4 It's our book.	The book is _____ .
5 It's _____ book.	The book is theirs.

whose and possessive *'s*

3 (Circle) **the correct words and complete the rule.**

A [1]*Whose / Who* son is Bart?
B Bart is [2]*Homer's / Homers'* son.
A [3]*Whose / Who's* Lisa's mom?
B Marge.

> **RULE:** To ask about possession, use the question word [1]_____ .
> To talk about possession, add [2]_____ to the end of a name / noun.
> If the name / noun ends in an *-s*, add the apostrophe (') after the *-s*.

4 (Circle) **the correct words.**

1 A *Whose / Who* phone is this?
  B Ask Jenny. I think it's *her / hers*.
2 Hey! That's *my / mine* sandwich, not *your / yours*.
3 I'm sure that's *Kate's / Kates'* bike. It looks just like *her / hers*.
4 A *Whose / Who* do you sit next to in math?
  B *Rafael / Rafael's*.
5 A Is that your *parent's / parents'* dog?
  B Yes, I think it's *their / theirs*.

> Workbook page 36

VOCABULARY
Family members

1 **Read the text. Complete the spaces in the picture with the missing family words.**

Here's a picture of my dad's side of the family. My dad has a *big* brother named Bob. He's my *uncle*, and he's great. He's so funny. His wife Nora is my *aunt*, and she's my dad's *sister-in-law*. She's also really nice. They have two sons – Jimmy and his *little* brother Robin. They're my *cousins*.

Of course, my dad and Bob have the same mom and dad. They are my *grandparents*. I call them *Grandma Diana* and *Grandpa Roger*. They're really nice to me because I'm their only granddaughter.

2 **SPEAKING** **Work in pairs. How many sentences can you make about the family in two minutes?**

> *Diana is Roger's wife.*

> *Jimmy is Nora's son.*

> Workbook page 38

my dad   [0] *Grandpa* Roger   [1]_____ Diana

Dad's [2]_____ brother
My [3]_____ Bob

Jimmy's [5]_____ brother
Robin (my [6]_____)

My [4]_____
Nora

My [7]_____
Jimmy

LISTENING

1 **Read and match three of the sentences with the pictures. Write the numbers in the boxes.**

WHY MY FAMILY DRIVES ME CRAZY

1 My sister always wants to borrow my clothes. It drives me crazy. (Lucy, 17)

2 My uncle tells really bad jokes. No one ever laughs – just him. (Howard, 15)

3 My dad never buys me new things. He's so mean. (Suzie, 16)

4 My grandpa just talks about the "good old days." I'm not really interested. (Viv, 12)

5 I often fight with my parents about going out. They always want me to stay at home. (Tom, 14)

6 My brother plays games all day. He never lets me play. (Paul, 14)

2 ◀)) **1.41** **Listen to the conversations. What is the relationship between the speakers?**

Conversation 1: _____

Conversation 2: _____

3 ◀)) **1.41** **Listen again and answer the questions.**

1 What does Lucy's sister Kathy want to borrow?

2 Why does she want to borrow it?

3 Does Lucy say yes or no?

4 Where does Tom want to go?

5 What does his mom say?

6 What does his dad say?

Pronunciation

Saying -er

Go to page 120. ◀))

FUNCTIONS
Asking for permission

1 **Complete the sentences from the listening.**

Asking for permission	Saying yes	Saying no
1_____ I borrow your yellow and black shirt? 2_____ I go out tonight?	Of course you can.	No, you 3_____.

2 **Write a short conversation for the picture in your notebook.**

3 **Think of requests that you make to different members of your family. Write them down.**

1 Can I borrow _____?

2 Can I go _____?

3 Can I have _____?

4 Can I play _____?

4 **Read them to your partner. Can he/she guess who you say this to?**

READING

1 Look at the photos. How do you think these girls were heroes? Read the article and find out.

THE SWIMMING POOL HEROES

Miya Peyregne, age nine, and her six-year-old sister, Tiffany, were in the swimming pool in the backyard of their house in the state of Michigan in the U.S. Their father, David, was with them. It was a beautiful day. There wasn't a cloud in the sky.

Suddenly, David shouted. He was in trouble. It was his legs. His legs weren't right. He was in pain.

Then he was under the water. The girls weren't scared, but they were worried. Was it just a joke or was he really in trouble? Twenty seconds later he was still under the water. Now Miya was scared.

There was no time to wait. In seconds Miya was under the water with her father. He was heavy, but with the help of the water she was able to pull him to one side of the pool. Now his head was out of the water. He was alive, but he wasn't conscious.

There was a cell phone in the house. Tiffany called 911 – the number for emergency services. Ten minutes later an ambulance was there. Soon their father was conscious again. The girls were relieved.

David still doesn't know what was wrong with his legs on that day. But he knows that his daughters were heroes and thanks them every day for saving his life. He is a very proud father.

2 Read the article again. Put the sentences in the correct order. There is one thing not mentioned in the article. Where do you think it goes?

a Miya goes under the water to help her dad. ☐
b Tiffany calls for an ambulance. ☐
c Their mother arrives home. ☐
d David has a problem with his legs. ☐
e David disappears under the water. ☐
f Miya and Tiffany are swimming with their dad, David. ☐

■ TRAIN TO THiNK

Making inferences

1 Work in pairs. Who says these sentences? Mark them M (Miya), T (Tiffany), or D (Dad).

1 "Help. I'm in trouble." ☐
2 "What's wrong, Dad?" ☐
3 "Help him. Go under the water." ☐
4 "Call an ambulance." ☐
5 "My dad needs help." ☐
6 "My heroes." ☐

2 Work in pairs. Write one more thing that each person might say.

1 Miya: _____
2 Tiffany: _____
3 David: _____
4 The ambulance driver: _____
5 The girls' mother: _____

3 **SPEAKING** Tell your ideas to another pair for them to guess.

I think Miya says that.

GRAMMAR
was / were

1 **Look at the examples from the article on page 42.** Circle **the correct words.**

1 It *was / were* a beautiful day. There *wasn't / weren't* a cloud in the sky.

2 The girls *were / weren't* scared, but they *were / weren't* worried.

3 *Was / Were* he really in trouble?

2 **Complete the table.**

Positive	Negative
I/he/she/it [0] ___was___	I/he/she/it [1] _____ (was not)
You/we/they [0] ___were___	You/we/they [2] _____ (were not)

Questions	Short answers
[3] _____ I/he/she/it?	Yes, I/he/she/it [4] _____ . No, I/he/she/it [5] _____ .
[6] _____ you/we/they?	Yes, you/we/they [7] _____ . No, you/we/they [8] _____ .

3 **Complete the questions and answers with *was, were, wasn't,* or *weren't*.**

1 A _____ you in bed at 9 p.m. last night?
  B No, I _____ . I _____ in the kitchen with my mom and dad.

2 A _____ your teacher happy with your homework?
  B Yes, she _____ . She _____ very happy with it.

3 A _____ it hot yesterday?
  B No, it _____ . It _____ really cold.

4 A _____ we at school yesterday?
  B No, we _____ . It _____ Sunday!

5 A _____ your parents born in the U.S.?
  B No, they _____ . They _____ born in Ecuador.

4 **SPEAKING** **Work in pairs. Ask and answer the questions in Exercise 3.**

Workbook page 37

VOCABULARY
Feelings

1 **Match the sentences.**

1 Our daughter was first in the race.
2 It was 9 p.m. and Mom wasn't home.
3 That wasn't a nice thing to say to Mimi.
4 Math class today was really difficult.
5 I wasn't expecting a big party.
6 The students were really noisy.
7 It was a really good horror movie.
8 What? The answer isn't 58?

a She's really **upset** now.
b And the teacher was **angry**.
c I was very **surprised** to see so many people there.
d I'm really **confused**. Please explain it again.
e We are so **proud** of her.
f I was **relieved** when it was over.
g I was really **worried**. Where was she?
h I was so **scared** at the end of it.

2 **Match the sentences in Exercise 1 with the pictures. Write the numbers 1–8.**

Workbook page 38

A ▢   B ▢   C ▢   D ▢

z+x(9x+7z)=25y + 4z

E ▢   F ▢   G ▢   H ▢

Culture

1 Look at the photos. What can you see? What's the same in the two photos?

2 🔊 1.44 Read and listen to the article. Which countries do the photos show?

3 Do people celebrate Children's Day in your country? If so, how do they celebrate it?

Around the world on Children's Day

In 1954 the United Nations started the first Universal Children's Day on November 20. It is to celebrate children all over the world. This is an international celebration of children, but now many countries around the world also have their own day each year when they celebrate their children.

June 1

CHINA: This is a very special day in schools. They take the children on camping trips or to the movies. Many children also get presents from their parents.

April 23

TURKEY: This day is a **national** holiday in Turkey. On this day, Turkey invites groups of children from other countries to stay with Turkish families and celebrate with them.

July 24

VANUATU: Children spend the morning at school where they celebrate and have fun. At noon, the children are free to go home and spend the rest of the day with their parents. Some parents buy their children a present, but the most important thing is for children and parents to have some time to spend **together**.

April 30

MEXICO: Children's Day is called *El Día Del Niño*. Some schools close for the day, and other schools have a special day for the children when they play games. The children also bring in their favorite food to **share** with their friends.

October 12

BRAZIL: This day is an important holiday in Brazil. Parents give their children many special **presents**. In some families, Children's Day is even bigger than Christmas.

May 5

JAPAN: To celebrate their special day, children fly carp streamers – big wind socks that look like fish. The official Children's Day, called *kodomo no hi*, is on May 5. But some people celebrate it on two days: March 3 for girls and May 5 for boys.

November 14

INDIA: Indians chose this day to celebrate because it is the birthday of the country's first Prime Minister, Jawaharlal Nehru. Nehru was famous for his love of children. On this day, the children plan the celebrations at their school. Their teachers sing and dance for the students.

4 Read the article again. Answer the questions in your notebook. Sometimes there is more than one correct answer.

In which country …

1 do the children spend more time with their mom and dad?
2 do they have more than one Children's Day?
3 is Children's Day also a famous person's birthday?
4 do children get presents?
5 do children celebrate with children from other countries?
6 do children celebrate Children's Day at school?

5 SPEAKING Work in small groups. Talk about the perfect Children's Day.

> All children get a big present.   School is closed for the whole day.
> Mom and Dad do your homework.

6 VOCABULARY There are six words in bold in the article. Match the words with these meanings. Write the words.

0 to have fun or do something special for example on a friend's birthday — *celebrate*
1 with other people _____
2 for a whole country _____
3 to have something at the same time with other people _____
4 for two or more countries _____
5 something you give to a person on a special day _____

WRITING
An invitation

1 Read the emails. Answer the questions.

1 Who is Dana?
2 Can Liam go to the party?

To: Liam_Walker@email.com
Subject: Party!

Hi Liam,
Would you like to come to my house next Friday for a party at 7 p.m.? It's my cousin Dana's birthday.
My address is 32 Lime Street. Make a playlist, please. I love your music.
Hope you can come. Let me know soon.
Tina
PS Don't tell Dana. It's a surprise.

To: TinaB@email.com
Subject: Re: Party!

Hi Tina,
I'd love to come to your party on Friday, but I have a small problem. I have soccer practice from 6 to 7:30 p.m. Can I come a little late? Is that OK?
No problem with the playlist. I have some great new songs.
See you Friday.
Liam

2 Match the sentences with the same meaning. Write a–e in the boxes.

1 Would you like to come to my party? ☐
2 I'd love to come to your party. ☐
3 I'm sorry, I can't come to your party. ☐
4 Make a playlist, please. ☐
5 Don't tell Dana. ☐

a I don't want Dana to know.
b Can you make a playlist?
c Can you come to my party?
d I'd love to come, but I can't.
e I'd be very happy to accept your invitation.

3 Which pairs of sentences in Exercise 2 can you use to do these things?

1 give an order _____
2 accept an invitation _____
3 make a special request _____
4 make an invitation _____
5 refuse an invitation _____

4 Read the invitation again. Answer the questions.

1 What is the invitation for?
2 What special requests does Tina make?

5 You want to invite a friend to your house. What information should you include? Check (✓) the correct answers.

1 your address ☐
2 how many brothers and sisters you have ☐
3 the time you want them to come ☐
4 the reason ☐
5 who your favorite singer is ☐
6 the day or date you want them to come ☐

6 Write an invitation (50 words). Choose one of these reasons. Include a special request or instruction.

- It's your birthday.
- You want to show a movie on your big new TV.
- You have a new computer game and want to play it.

CAMBRIDGE ENGLISH: Key

■ THiNK EXAMS

READING AND WRITING
Part 2: Multiple-choice sentence completion Workbook page 61

1   Read the sentences about a trip to a café. Choose the best word (A, B, or C) for each space.

0	I got 99% on my math test! Mom is really _____ .	(A) proud	B scared	C upset
1	She takes me and my little _____ to the café for ice cream.	A uncle	B aunt	C sister
2	I eat _____ of ice cream.	A many	B any	C a lot
3	My mom doesn't want her ice cream, so I eat _____ , too.	A her	B mine	C hers
4	And then I drink _____ soda.	A not enough	B too many	C too much
5	I _____ feel very well, so we go home.	A not	B don't	C am not

Part 3: Dialogue matching Workbook page 35

2   Complete the conversation. What does Anita say to the waiter?

For questions 1–5, choose the correct letter A–H.

WAITER	Can I help you?	A	How much is it?
ANITA	(0) _G_	B	Orange juice, please.
WAITER	Of course, here you are.	C	I'd like a cheese omelette, please.
(5 minutes later)		D	And the orange juice.
WAITER	OK, so what can I get you?	E	Can I have the check?
ANITA	(1) _____	F	No, thanks. Just the omelette.
WAITER	OK. Would you like an appetizer?	G	~~I'd like to see the menu, please.~~
ANITA	(2) _____	H	Yes, please. Can I have some strawberry ice cream?
WAITER	And what would you like to drink?		
ANITA	(3) _____		
WAITER	And would you like a dessert?		
ANITA	(4) _____		
WAITER	OK, so that's a cheese omelette and strawberry ice cream.		
(20 minutes later)			
ANITA	(5) _____		
WAITER	Of course. I'll be back soon.		

LISTENING
Part 3: Three-option multiple-choice Workbook page 43

3   ◀))1.45 Listen to Jessica talking to Brandon about her family. For each question, choose the right answer (A, B, or C).

0	The party was last	(A) Friday evening.	B Saturday evening.	C Friday afternoon.
1	The party was for Brandon's	A brother.	B dad.	C uncle.
2	Brandon's uncle is	A 20.	B 34.	C 44.
3	Brandon's aunt is named	A Anna.	B Carla.	C Ruth.
4	Mike is Brandon's	A brother.	B dad.	C cousin.
5	Brandon has	A two sisters.	B one sister.	C one sister and one brother.

TEST YOURSELF

VOCABULARY

1 Complete the sentences with the words in the list. There are two extra words.

angry | big | boiled | grilled | relieved | scared
grandparents | carrots | confused | spicy | chicken | proud

1 I don't like many vegetables – just peppers and _____ .
2 I was worried about the exam, so I was _____ when I did well on it.
3 The chili is too _____ . I can't eat it.
4 It was a really stupid thing to do. My parents were really _____ with me.
5 To make _____ potatoes you need to cook them in water for about 20 minutes.
6 There was a strange noise outside the house. We were very _____ .
7 Nathan's a vegetarian. He doesn't eat _____ .
8 I don't really understand this homework. I'm a little _____ .
9 Freddie's my _____ brother. I'm 14, and he's 20.
10 My mom's mother and father are my _____ .

/10

GRAMMAR

2 Complete the sentences with the words in the list.

much | many | ours | our | was | were

1 How _____ sugar do you want in your coffee?
2 It _____ really cold yesterday.
3 That's not your dog. It's _____ .
4 There are too _____ people in here. I can't find him.
5 _____ dog's named Spike.
6 Where _____ you last night?

3 Find and correct the mistake in each sentence.

1 This salad has too much beans.   _____
2 That's not your sandwich. It's my.   _____
3 My parents was very proud of my grades in school. _____
4 I like Clara, and I really like hers sister, too. _____
5 How many water do you want?   _____
6 I think this is Kevins' book.   _____

/12

FUNCTIONAL LANGUAGE

4 Write the missing words.

1 A I'm late. I'm really _____ .
   B Don't _____ . We still have lots of time.
2 A I _____ this question is really difficult.
   B I think _____ , too.
3 A _____ I borrow your bike, Dad?
   B Of _____ you can.
4 A Can I go _____ tonight?
   B No, you _____ .

/8

MY SCORE   /30

| 22 – 30 |
| 10 – 21 |
| 0 – 9 |

5 | IT FEELS LIKE HOME

OBJECTIVES

FUNCTIONS: talking about events in the past; making suggestions

GRAMMAR: simple past (regular verbs); modifiers: *very*, *really*, *pretty*; simple past negative

VOCABULARY: parts of a house; furniture; adjectives with *-ed / -ing*; phrasal verbs with *look*

A

B

C

D

E

F

READING

1 🔊1.46 Match the words in the list with the photos. Write 1–6 in the boxes. Then listen and check.

1 kitchen | 2 bedroom | 3 bathroom
4 living room | 5 dining room | 6 yard

2 Match the verbs with the places in Exercise 1.

eat _____ cook _____ watch TV _____
sleep _____ bathe _____ play soccer _____

3 SPEAKING Work in pairs. Do you have the same ideas? What other activities do you do in these places?

> I talk to my dad in the kitchen.

> I sing in the bathroom.

4 SPEAKING Look at the photos on page 49. What can you say about the house?

5 🔊1.47 Read and listen to the magazine article. Choose the correct options A, B, or C.

1 The line of people wanted to help James May buy a house.
 A Right B Wrong C Doesn't say

2 They finished building the house in one month.
 A Right B Wrong C Doesn't say

3 The LEGO fridge worked.
 A Right B Wrong C Doesn't say

4 James May liked the bed.
 A Right B Wrong C Doesn't say

5 There were photos of the house on a Facebook page.
 A Right B Wrong C Doesn't say

6 A charity for children has the LEGOs now.
 A Right B Wrong C Doesn't say

The LEGO® house

A few years ago in August, there was a very long line of people in the countryside near London, England. Some people started waiting in line at 4:30 in the morning. Why were they there? They wanted to help James May, a TV host, build a house. But this was not an ordinary house. This was a LEGO house.

Together, 1,200 people used 3.3 million (yes, 3,300,000) LEGOs to make a real house.

It was part of a TV show called *Toy Stories*. On the show, James May used traditional toys to make "real" things. Why LEGOs? Well, because when he was young, James May loved LEGOs and played with them all the time.

The people finished building the house on September 17, almost seven weeks after they started. Everything was LEGO. All the walls, doors, and windows were LEGO. There was a LEGO bedroom and a LEGO bed. There was a LEGO bathroom with a LEGO toilet and shower – and they worked! In the kitchen there was a LEGO fridge (but no stove), and there were LEGO tables and chairs. There was even a LEGO cat. James May stayed in the house one night and was surprised because the bed was pretty comfortable.

At first, a theme park called LEGOLAND planned to buy the house, but later they decided not to. James May tried to find another buyer. He started a Facebook page and asked other people to buy it, but nobody wanted it. So on September 22, they started to take the house apart. A few days later, there wasn't a LEGO house anymore.

James May was not happy about it because more than 1,000 people worked hard to build the house and everything inside it. Other people were not so sad. The television company donated the three million LEGOs to a charity for children.

■ THiNK VALUES ■

Community spirit

1 Read what people said about the LEGO house. Match the social values a–d with the comments 1–4.

a working together   c having fun
b being creative   d caring for others

1 *We really enjoyed this – we laughed a lot.* ☐

2 *The idea of building a LEGO cat was really interesting.* ☐

3 *I loved being with so many people doing the same thing!* ☐

4 *I think it's great that they donated the LEGOs to a charity for children.* ☐

2 SPEAKING Put the values a–d in Exercise 1 in order of importance for you. Compare your ideas with a partner.

I think working together is really important. It's my number 1.

Me, too. It's my number 2.

What's your number 1?

Caring for others.

GRAMMAR
Simple past (regular verbs)

1 Find the simple past forms of these verbs in the article and write them below. Then complete the rules.

0	start	_started_	5	stay _____
1	want	_____	6	plan _____
2	use	_____	7	decide _____
3	finish	_____	8	try _____
4	work	_____	9	ask _____

RULE: Use the simple past to talk about finished actions in the past.

With regular verbs:

- We usually add ¹_____ to the verb (e.g., *start – started / stay – stayed*).
- If the verb ends in *-e* (e.g., *use*), we add ²_____ .
- If a short verb ends in consonant + vowel + consonant (e.g., *plan*), we ³_____ the final consonant and add *-ed* (e.g., *planned*).
- We add *-ed* to verbs ending in vowel + *-y* (e.g., *played*).
- If the verb ends in consonant + *-y* (e.g., *try*), we change the *y* to ⁴_____ and add ⁵_____ .

2 Complete the sentences. Use the simple past form of the verbs.

0 When my grandfather was young, he _____*played*_____ (play) with LEGOs all the time.

1 We _____ (start) to paint our house last month, and we _____ (finish) yesterday.

2 I _____ (decide) to change my bedroom, so I _____ (paint) the walls pink.

3 We _____ (try) to find another house last year because we _____ (want) to move.

4 I _____ (visit) my aunt and uncle because they _____ (want) to show me their new apartment.

5 My parents _____ (study) lots of ideas for a new kitchen before they _____ (order) it.

6 On my last vacation, I _____ (stay) with my grandparents and _____ (help) them clean up the yard.

Workbook page 46 ▶

Pronunciation
Regular past tense endings /d/, /t/, /ɪd/

Turn to page 120. 🔊

VOCABULARY
Furniture

1 🔊1.50 **Match the words with the photos. Write 1–12 in the boxes. Then listen and check.**

1 chair | 2 carpet | 3 stove | 4 curtains
5 desk | 6 lamp | 7 mirror | 8 shelves
9 shower | 10 sofa | 11 toilet | 12 dresser

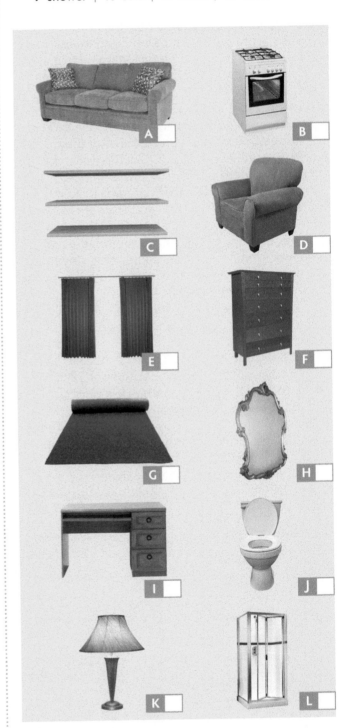

2 SPEAKING **Work in pairs. Where are these things in your home? Tell your partner.**

> *There are mirrors in our bathroom, in my parents' bedroom, and in our living room.*

Workbook page 48 ▶

LISTENING

1 SPEAKING Work in pairs. Describe the pictures.

1 _____

2 _____

3 _____

4 _____

2 🔊 1.51 Listen to four people talking about "home." Write the names under the correct pictures.

Carlos | Marta | Jacob | Emma

3 🔊 1.51 Listen again. Complete the table with the missing information.

	Where's home for you?	What I like doing there
Emma	Home is where I feel ¹_____ .	²_____
Jacob	Somewhere ³_____ .	⁴_____
Marta	Our ⁵_____ kitchen.	⁶_____
Carlos	My ⁷_____ .	⁸_____

GRAMMAR
Modifiers: *very, really, pretty*

1 Write the name of the person from Exercise 3 who says these things. Then underline the words before the adjectives and complete the rule.

1 I feel really happy there. _____

2 Our kitchen is pretty small. _____

3 The chair is very comfortable. _____

> **RULE:** We use the words *very, really,* and *pretty* to say more about an adjective.
> - The words *very* and ¹_____ are used to make an adjective stronger.
> - The word ²_____ usually means "a little."

2 Write true sentences about you. Use the words.

0 kitchen – big / small
Our kitchen isn't very big / is pretty small.

1 bedroom – clean / messy

2 sofa – comfortable / uncomfortable

3 home – busy / quiet   →Workbook page 47

■ THiNK SELF-ESTEEM ■
Feeling safe

1 Think about the questions and take notes.

a Where do you feel "at home"? Describe the place.

b What's most important for you there? (furniture? things? colors? people?)

c What does that place feel like for you? (relaxing? safe? comfortable?)

2 SPEAKING Write two or three sentences about where you feel at home. Read them aloud in groups.

> *I feel at home in my bedroom. My bed is pretty small, but it's very comfortable. I like lying on it and thinking about my life.*

> *I feel at home when I'm with my family. My mom and dad are great, and my brother is my best friend. I love doing things with them.*

> *I feel at home in the living room. Our sofa is really comfortable. I love sitting there on my own reading a good book.*

READING

1 Read Hillary's vacation blog. Complete the sentences with a word or a number.

DAY 5

Dad gets it right! (finally)

Day five of the Italian adventure and we're in Naples. We arrived here early yesterday morning, but as usual we were only at the hotel for about five minutes before Dad wanted to take us somewhere. This time it was to the ancient city of Pompeii. I didn't really want to go. I wanted to go shoe shopping.

We traveled there by train. The trip didn't take long – but long enough for Dad to tell us a bit about the history. Many years ago, Pompeii was a large Roman city near a volcano called Mount Vesuvius. Then, on August 24, 79 CE, the volcano erupted and completely covered the city in ash. It killed about 20,000 people. But the ash didn't destroy the buildings, and now, almost 2,000 years later, you can walk around the city and see how people lived all those years ago.

2,000-year-old houses? At first I thought, "Thanks, Dad. Really boring." But I was wrong! The houses were very interesting. Most of them were really big with lots of rooms (so lots of space to get away from annoying brothers and sisters!). There were paintings and mosaics all over the walls. I'd love a Roman mosaic of One Direction on my bedroom wall. Also, I was amazed at the bathrooms. I'd love a big bathroom in our house – ours is so small!

I got really interested in Pompeii. I wasn't bored at all. In fact, I have lots of ideas for our house when we get home!

Mount Vesuvius – a real ¹_____ . (I hope it doesn't erupt!)

About ²_____ people died here, all of them covered in ash.

The paintings and ³_____ are really beautiful.

The houses are about ⁴_____ years old.

2 Answer the questions.

1 Where did Hillary's family go?
2 How did they get to Pompeii?
3 What did Hillary's dad tell them about on the way there?
4 When did Vesuvius erupt?
5 What did Hillary think about Pompeii at first?
6 What did Hillary like about Pompeii?

WRITING

Use your answers in Exercise 2 to write a summary of the text in no more than 100 words.

Hillary went to Pompeii and ...

GRAMMAR
Simple past negative

1 **Compete the sentences from Hillary's blog and complete the rule.**

1 I _____ really want to go.
2 The trip _____ take long.
3 The ash _____ destroy the buildings.

> **RULE:** To make any verb negative in the simple past, use _____ + the base form of the verb.

2 **Here are some more things Hillary wrote about Pompeii. Make them negative.**

0 We visited all of the houses.
We didn't visit all of the houses.
1 I wanted to go home.
2 The poor people lived in big houses.
3 Dad ordered a pizza for lunch.
4 It rained in the afternoon.

3 **SPEAKING** **Work in pairs. Tell your partner two things that you did and two things that you didn't do last weekend. Choose from the verbs in the list.**

work | climb | play | travel | clean
help | study | use | dance | walk

> *I didn't watch TV.*

> *I visited my friends.*

> Workbook page 47

VOCABULARY
adjectives with -ed and -ing

1 **How does Hillary feel? Write the adjectives under the photos.**

annoyed | relaxed | bored | interested | amazed

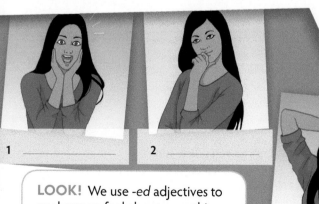

1 _____   2 _____

> **LOOK!** We use -ed adjectives to say how we feel about something.
> We use -ing adjectives to say what we think about something or to describe something.

2 **What did Hillary say about Pompeii? Complete the sentences with *interested* or *interesting*.**

1 I got really _____ in Pompeii.
2 The houses were very _____ .

3 **Circle the correct words.**

1 I get *annoyed / annoying* when people ignore me.
2 His painting was excellent. I was *amazed / amazing*.
3 Luis talks about soccer all the time! He's really *bored / boring*.
4 A hot shower is always very *relaxed / relaxing*.
5 I think math class is really *interested / interesting*.

4 **Complete the sentences so that they are true for you.**

1 I think _____ is really annoying.
2 _____ is the most amazing singer.
3 I'm really interested in _____ .
4 I'm never bored when _____
_____ .

5 **SPEAKING** **Work in pairs. Compare your answers.**

> Workbook page 48

WRITING
A blog post

1 **Think about a real vacation or an invented vacation. Take notes about these questions.**

a Where did you go?
b Who did you go with?
c What did you do that was very special / different?
d What did you like / not like about the vacation?
e What was *boring / exciting / amazing / interesting / annoying* about the vacation?

2 **Use your notes from Exercise 1 to write a blog post about your vacation. Write 120–150 words. Write three paragraphs.**

Paragraph 1 – your answers to a and b
Paragraph 2 – your answer to c
Paragraph 3 – your answers to d and e

3 _____
4 _____
5 _____

Hey, look at that guy!

1 **Look at the photos and answer the questions.**

What do you think the four friends are saying about the man? What do they know about him?

2 🔊 1.52 **Now read and listen to the photostory to check your answers.**

RYAN Stop looking at your GPS – we know how to get to school.
OLIVIA Very funny. Hey, look at that guy!
RYAN What about him?
MEGAN I think he was here yesterday, too.

LUKE So? A homeless guy. What's the big deal?
RYAN Yeah, right.
OLIVIA He has problems. Don't you care?
RYAN Well, to be honest – no, not very much.

MEGAN But it's really sad!
OLIVIA I know what you mean. I watched a show on TV a while ago about homeless people. Awful!
MEGAN Can you imagine? No place to live. It must be horrible.
RYAN Well, I'm sure that's true. But it's not really our problem.

OLIVIA Let's go and talk to him.
RYAN Hold on! Do you think that's a good idea?
MEGAN What do you mean? He's poor, but that doesn't mean he's dangerous.
LUKE OK, maybe not dangerous. He's probably not very nice, though.
OLIVIA Maybe he needs help.

DEVELOPING SPEAKING

3 Work in pairs. Discuss what happens next in the story. Write down your ideas.

We think the boys go to school but Megan and Olivia talk to the man.

4 ▶ EP3 Watch to find out how the story continues.

5 Put the sentences in the correct order. Write 1–8 in the boxes.

- a The students decide to ask somebody from a charity for help.
- b The girls are worried about the man.
- c When they go back to the park, the man gives Olivia her necklace.
- [1] d The friends are on their way to school.
- e Other students start laughing at her.
- f Ryan tells the other students about the homeless person.
- g In the park, they see a homeless person.
- h The teacher notices that Olivia is not paying attention.

PHRASES FOR FLUENCY

1 Find these expressions in the story. Who says them?

- a What's the big deal? _____
- b …, to be honest, … _____
- c I know what you mean. _____
- d …, it's not our problem. _____
- e Hold on! _____
- f …, though. _____

2 Use the expressions in Exercise 1 to complete the dialogues. Write a–f.

1 A She's usually a nice girl. Sometimes she gets really angry, _____ .
  B _____ . Yesterday she yelled at me for no reason!

2 A I need help. You guys have to help me with my homework!
  B _____ ! It's *your* homework – so really, _____ .

3 A It's only a small test tomorrow. Ten questions. _____ ? Right?
  B Well, _____ , I'm a little worried about it.

WordWise
Phrasal verbs with *look*

1 Look at these sentences from the story. Complete them with the words from the list.

up | for | at | into

1 Hey, look _____ that guy.
2 I'm just looking it _____ on my phone.
3 We need to look _____ why he's homeless.
4 Let's look _____ him.

2 Circle the correct word in each dialogue.

1 A Why are you looking *for / at* me like that?
  B Because I'm angry with you.
2 A I can't find my pen.
  B I'll help you look *at / for* it.
3 A Do the police know what happened?
  B No, they are still looking *for / into* it.
4 A What does this word mean?
  B I don't know. Let's look it *at / up* in the dictionary.

Workbook page 48

FUNCTIONS
Making suggestions

1 Complete the sentences from the story with words from the lists. Then write ✓ (agree), ✗ (disagree), or ? (uncertain).

A ~~How~~ | could | Let's | Why
B ~~idea~~ | do | great | sure

0 A *How* about asking our parents for money?
  B I don't think that's a good *idea* . ✗

1 A _____ don't we try and help him?
  B Let's _____ that. _____

2 A _____ give him our school lunch.
  B I'm not so _____ about that. _____

3 A We _____ take him something after school.
  B I think that's a _____ idea. _____

At a market

2 ROLE PLAY Work in pairs. Student A: Go to page 127. Student B: Go to page 128. Take two or three minutes to prepare. Then have a conversation.

6 BEST FRIENDS

OBJECTIVES

FUNCTIONS: talking about past events; talking about what you like doing

GRAMMAR: simple past (irregular verbs); double genitive; simple past questions

VOCABULARY: past time expressions; character adjectives

READING

1 SPEAKING Look at the photos. Say what the people are doing.

> They're surfing the Internet.

2 SPEAKING Match these words with the photos and compare with a partner. (Some words go with more than one photo.)

alone | together | happy
sad | bored | excited

> In photo 1, they're together and they're excited.

3 SPEAKING Work in pairs. Talk about things you like doing alone and other things you like doing with other people. Here are some ideas to help you.

watch a movie | walk | do homework | study
read | have breakfast | go shopping

> I like going shopping with friends. I don't like going alone! I like doing homework alone.

4 Look at the pictures on page 57. How do you think the best friends met? How do they communicate now?

5 🔊 1.53 Read and listen to the web article. Check your ideas.

6 Read the article again. Choose the correct answers.

1 Sarah and Paige talk online every *day / week*.

2 Paige lives in *Europe / New Zealand* and Sarah lives in the *U.S. / U.K.*

3 Their mothers found each other when Sarah and Paige were *babies / teenagers*.

4 Sarah gave Paige a lot of *photos / confidence*.

5 The girls finally met in *the U.S. / New Zealand*.

6 Sarah thinks she and Paige *will / won't* always be best friends.

Best friends ... 8,000 miles apart

Sarah and Paige are best friends. Like many teenage girls, they talk about school, fashion, sports, and family, and they are together online and on the phone every day. "We talk about boys and life and compare things," says Sarah.

The girls have a very typical friendship, but there is one difference. Paige lives in New Zealand, and Sarah lives in the U.S., 8,000 miles away. They talk on the phone and send emails, but they can only see each other on video chat.

The girls first "met" when they were babies. Sarah was born with only one arm, and her mother wanted to meet parents of similar children. She found Paige's mother on the Internet and learned that Paige also had only one arm. The girls' parents shared letters and photos.

Later, Paige and Sarah became friends over email. "I needed someone that could understand everything about me," says Sarah. They talk about typical teenage things, and they also share their feelings about living with one arm. They show each other how to do things that are difficult with one arm, such as painting their fingernails. "Sarah taught me a lot," says Paige, "and gave me a lot of confidence. I can tell Sarah things that I wouldn't tell my other friends. I trust her with my life."

Finally, after they were best friends for eight years, Sarah flew to New Zealand to meet Paige for the first time. When she finally saw Paige, she ran to her best friend, and the two girls hugged and cried. The first thing Sarah said to Paige was, "You're so beautiful." "So are you," said Paige.

"Some best friends come and go," says Sarah. "Paige will always be my best friend."

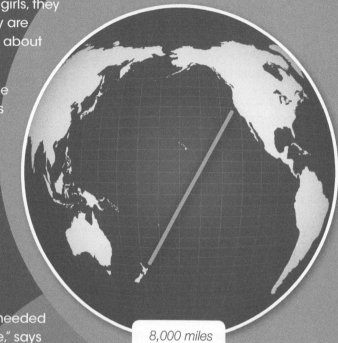

8,000 miles

■ THiNK VALUES ■

Friendship and loyalty

1 **Choose the best way to finish this sentence.**

   I think this story tells us that it is most important to …
   1 … help your friends.
   2 … look good.
   3 … know people similar to you.
   4 … share your feelings with people.
   5 … have lots and lots of friends.
   6 … have one good friend.

2 **Compare your ideas with a partner.**

3 **SPEAKING** **Choose three of the values in Exercise 1. Put them in order of importance for you (1, 2, 3). Then compare with others.**

   For me, to help your friends is number 1.

   That's my number 3. I think it's more important to have a best friend.

GRAMMAR
Simple past (irregular verbs)

1 **Look at these sentences about the article on page 57. All the verbs are in the simple past. How are the verbs in 1 different from the verbs in 2?**

   1 The parents **wanted** to meet.
     They **shared** letters.

   2 They **met** as babies.
     She **taught** her a lot.

2 **Look back at the article on page 57. Write the simple past forms of these verbs.**

0	meet	_met_	4	give	_____
1	find	_____	5	fly	_____
2	become	_____	6	see	_____
3	teach	_____	7	say	_____

3 **Find at least two more irregular simple past forms in the article. Write the verbs.**

   _____ _____

4 **Correct these two sentences about the article. Make them negative.**

   1 They became friends in school.

     _____

   2 Their parents cried.

     _____

5 **Look at the pictures and the cues and write the sentences in the simple past.**

Workbook page 54

VOCABULARY
Past time expressions

1 **Complete the series with words from the list.**

   a year | morning | month

   When we talk about the past, we often use expressions like these:

   - yesterday, yesterday [1]_____ , yesterday afternoon
   - last night, last week, last [2]_____ , last December
   - an hour ago, two weeks ago, a month ago, [3]_____ ago

2 **Complete the sentences with your own information. Use irregular verbs.**

   1 A year ago, I _____.
   2 Ten years ago, I _____.
   3 Last year, I _____.
   4 Yesterday morning, I _____.
   5 Last night, I _____.

3 **Complete the sentences with a time expression with *ago*.**

   0 Andy is twenty. He left school when he was eighteen.
     Andy left school two years ago.

   1 It's eight o'clock. I had breakfast at seven o'clock.
     I had breakfast _____

   2 It's 10:20. The movie began at 10:00.
     The movie _____

   3 It's December. Your vacation was in July.
     My vacation _____

Workbook page 56

1 We / go / to Brazil, but we / go / to Rio.
  We went to Brazil, but we didn't go to Rio.

2 I / see / Marco, but I / see / Natalia.

3 Sue / come / to my party, but Dan / come.

4 I make / sandwiches, but I / make / cake.

LISTENING

1 **Which sentences do you agree with?**

1 Soccer players are never friends with players from other teams.

2 Soccer players never help other players.

3 Soccer players only want to win championships.

2 🔊 1.54 **Listen to a story about Cristiano Ronaldo. Check (✓) the correct box.**

The kids think the story is …

☐ certainly true.

☐ possibly true.

☐ certainly not true.

3 🔊 1.54 **Listen again and choose the right answer (A, B, or C).**

1 What was the last name of Ronaldo's friend?

A Albert

B The boy doesn't remember.

C The boy didn't find the name.

2 How many places were there at the soccer school?

A one B two C three

3 Why did Albert pass the ball to Cristiano?

A Because Albert wanted a friend.

B Because Albert was tired.

C Because Cristiano was a better player.

4 What was the final score of the game?

A 1–1 B 2–0 C 3–0

5 What is Albert's job now?

A He's a soccer player.

B We don't know.

C He drives cars.

6 What did Ronaldo give his friend?

A A car.

B A house.

C A car and a house.

4 SPEAKING **Work in pairs. Tell your partner about a great present someone gave you.**

> *Last year my … gave me a … . I was really happy / excited because … .*

GRAMMAR
Double genitive

1 **Read the sentence from the listening. Then choose the correct options to complete the rule.**

Ronaldo was there, and there was <u>a friend of his</u> *named Albert.*

RULE: We can form the "double genitive" in two ways:

● noun + of + possessive [1]*pronoun / adjective* (*mine, yours, his, hers, ours, yours, theirs*)

● noun + of + possessive adjective (*my, your, his, her, our, your, their*) + noun + possessive *'s*.

We use it to talk about [2]*one of many things / many things* that we have.

2 **Circle the correct words.**

0 She's a friend of *me / mine*.

1 Mr. Smith is a teacher of *my sister / my sister's*.

2 She's a cousin of *John / John's*.

3 Mrs. Jones is a neighbor of *ours / us*.

3 **Rewrite the underlined parts of the sentences.**

0 See that man? He's <u>my father's friend</u>.
He's *a friend of my father's* .

1 Steve and Angela are <u>our friends</u>.
Steve and Angela are _____ .

2 Mike borrowed <u>my shirt</u>.
Mike borrowed _____ .

3 I went on vacation with <u>my cousin</u>.
I went on vacation with _____ .

Workbook page 55 ➤

■ TRAIN TO THiNK ■
Making decisions

1 **Draw a mind map.**

● Complete the three circles with names of people who are close to you (friends, family).

● What do these people like? Write your ideas on the lines.

2 SPEAKING **Work in small groups. Imagine it's your friends' birthdays. What presents do you think they would like? Show your mind maps and make suggestions.**

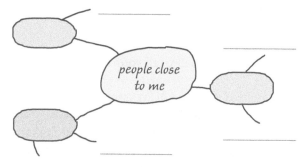

people close to me

READING

1 Read the magazine article quickly. Complete the sentences.

1 Richard and Sharon met for the first time on

_____ .

2 The second time they met, they went

_____ .

2 Read the article again. Put the events in the order they happened. Write the numbers 1–8.

- [ ] a Richard and Sharon go to a show together.
- [ ] b Richard has an accident.
- [ ] c Richard gives Sharon a present.
- [ ] d Sharon saves Richard's life.
- [ ] e Richard goes to the hospital.
- [ ] f Sharon calls Richard.
- [ ] g Richard goes surfing.
- [ ] h Richard sees Sharon for the first time.

3 SPEAKING Work in pairs. Tell the story. Use the ideas in Exercise 2 and the past tense.

> *Richard went surfing. He had an accident ...*

FUNCTIONS
Talking about past events

1 Think about when you made a new friend. Take notes.

- Who?
- When?
- Where?
- What happened?

2 SPEAKING In pairs, tell your story.

> *I met my friend Al five years ago. I was on vacation in Florida with my family. We were at a small hotel. Al's family was in the same hotel. We made friends on the first day and spent the whole vacation together.*

Real life

How we met

This week, lifeguard Sharon Evans and student Richard Lambert tell our reporter about their friendship and how they almost never met.

Q: *So first of all, when and where did you meet?*

Richard We first met in 2012, one morning about 10:30 on Bondi Beach, in Sydney.

Sharon Actually, we met in the water.

Q: *OK, so how did you meet?*

Richard I was out in the deep water on my surfboard when another board knocked me on the head. The next thing I knew, I was on the beach looking up at this face.

Sharon I was on the beach that day. I saw what happened, so I swam out and brought Richard back in. He was unconscious, but luckily I got him to start breathing again. But for a minute I thought he was dead.

Richard And then they took me to the hospital. I didn't have a chance to even say thanks to Sharon.

Q: *So what did you do?*

Richard There was a really big show the next week with a popular Belgian-Australian singer named Gotye. I bought two tickets for Sharon and left them at work for her a few days later. I thought she could take someone with her. I also left her a note to say thanks with my phone number on it.

Sharon He was really generous. They were expensive tickets.

Q: *Did you take a friend to the show?*

Sharon I didn't know who to take, and then I had a great idea.

Q: *What was it?*

Richard Well, when I got home from work that day there was a voicemail on my phone. It was Sharon. She invited me to go with her. We had a great time. She was so cheerful and easy-going. We became really good friends right away.

GRAMMAR
Simple past questions

1 **Put the words in order to make questions. Check your answers in the article on page 60.**

   1 do / did / what / you / ?　**2** did / you / meet / how / ?　**3** friend / show / take / you / a / to / did / the / ?

2 **Complete the table.**

Question	Answer
¹_____ I/you/he/she/we/they enjoy the show?	Yes, I/you/he/she/we/they ³_____ .
	No, I/you/he/she/we/they ⁴_____ (did not).
What time ²_____ I/you/he/she/we/they get home?	I/you/he/she/we/they ⁵_____ home at midnight.

3 **Match the questions and answers.**

   1 Did you have a good weekend? ____
   2 Did you play computer games yesterday? ____
   3 Where did you meet your best friend? ____
   4 Who did you text yesterday? ____
   5 What did you have for dinner last night? ____

   a Yes, I did. I completed four levels.
   b We met at school four years ago.
   c We had chicken and fries.
   d No, I didn't. It rained all the time.
   e I texted my best friend.

4 **SPEAKING Work in pairs. Ask the questions 1–5 and give your own answers.**　Workbook page 55 ➡

VOCABULARY
Character adjectives

Look at the pictures. Read the sentences and write the names under the people.

1 _____

2 _____

3 _____

4 _____

5 _____

6 _____

7 _____

8 _____

MY FRIENDS

- Nick is intelligent. He knows a lot about everything
- Maria is cheerful. She always has a smile on her face.
- Brandon is jealous. He's not happy when you talk to other friends.
- Ben is helpful. He's always ready to help you.
- Ruby is confident. She's not scared to talk in public.
- Liz is generous. She's always happy to share her things with you.
- Chloe is easy-going. She never gets angry about anything.
- Connor is funny. He always makes me laugh.

Pronunciation
Stressed syllables in words

Turn to page 120.　

Workbook page 56 ➡

Culture

1   Look at the photos of friends. Who's having a good time? Who's having a bad time?

2   🔊 1.57   Read and listen to the article. Five people commented on the different myths about friendship. Match the people to the myths.

Myth 1 _____   Myth 2 _____   Myth 3 _____

Myth 4 _____   Myth 5 _____

3   SPEAKING Which of the five people do you agree with? Who do you disagree with? Compare with others in the class.

Friendship myths

Everyone wants to have friends, and friendships are important to teenagers all over the world. However, when people start a friendship, they sometimes expect too much from it. Here are five things about friendship that some people believe are true. But in fact they aren't – they are myths.

We spoke to teens from different countries. Read what they think.

Myth no. 1:   Friends are there to make you happy.

Myth no. 2:   A real friend will never disappoint you.

Myth no. 3:   The more friends you have, the better.

Myth no. 4:   Friends share everything.

Myth no. 5:   If you have no friends, something's wrong with you.

Mei, Shanghai, China
Nobody's perfect, so why do we think friends can be perfect? We all make mistakes, so it's only normal that there are times when good friends make mistakes, too. Maybe you think that a really good friend always knows what you need. That's wrong – be careful! Sometimes you need to say to your friends, "Please do this" or "Don't do that." Don't forget that there are times when your friends are stressed or unhappy, too. Then they can't help you the way you would like them to.   **A**

Flávia, São Paulo, Brazil
There can be times in your life when you have a lot of friends, and other times when you only have one or two. Maybe you don't have any friends right now, for example, because you're in a new city or school. When you don't have any friends, it's important to wait and be patient. Make sure you're a friendly person – so other people want to make friends with you!   **B**

Daniel, Veracruz, Mexico
It takes time to build a good friendship. You don't want to tell your friend everything about yourself on the first day of your friendship. You and your friends want to share some things. But it's important to remember that there are other things that you don't want to share, and that's fine! Don't feel bad about it.   **C**

Fernanda, Quito, Ecuador
You want to be a good friend, right? To build a good friendship, it's important to have fun together, to listen to your friends when they have a problem, to help them when they need you, or just to go and watch a movie together, or play sports. And that takes time! That's why I think it's better to have one or two friends, not a lot of friends.   **D**

Alexsei, St Petersburg, Russia
It's not a good idea to wait for others to make you happy. There are times when you're happy and other times when you're sad. And when you're not happy, try to think, "What can I do to stop this? How can I help myself?" Friendship is a place to share happiness, but there may be times when you and your friends aren't happy. And that's OK.   **E**

4 Read the article again. Who has these ideas?

1 You need to have a good time with your friends. _____

2 You won't make friends if you are an unfriendly person. _____

3 We need to remember that our friends have bad days, too. _____

4 You don't have to tell your friends everything about you. _____

5 We won't always have the same number of friends in our life. _____

6 It's not always a good thing to have a lot of friends. _____

7 We shouldn't expect our friends to always get everything right. _____

8 We shouldn't always expect friends to make us happy. _____

9 You can't always expect your friends to be happy. _____

10 You can't make a really good friend quickly. _____

5 VOCABULARY **There are eight highlighted words in the article. Match the words with these meanings. Write the words.**

0 ideas that many people believe but that are not true _____*myths*_____

1 when you feel happy _____

2 the relationships you have with friends _____

3 show that you are not in a hurry and have time _____

4 worried, for example when you have too much homework _____

5 get to know and like a person _____

6 keep in your mind _____

7 at this moment _____

SPEAKING

1 Choose the words that make the sentences true for you.

1 When I'm sad, I want my friends to *listen to me / tell me a joke / leave me alone.*

2 When I'm happy, I want my friends to *watch a movie / play sports / listen to music / go shopping* with me.

2 Work with a partner. Read your sentences aloud and compare your answers.

WRITING
An apology

1 Read the message and think about the questions.

1 How does John feel, and why?

2 What does he want to do about it?

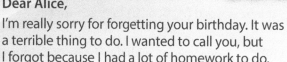

Dear Alice,

I'm really sorry for forgetting your birthday. It was a terrible thing to do. I wanted to call you, but I forgot because I had a lot of homework to do. I feel really bad. I'd like to see you soon to say sorry. I also have something I want to give you.

Can we meet up on Thursday?

John

2 Read the messages. Which is the answer to John?

Thanks for your message.

Don't worry about it. I'm not upset. And yes, I'd love to see you on Thursday. I can't wait to see what you have for me.

Thanks for the message.

I'm sorry I can't come to your birthday party on Thursday, but I'm really busy. Have fun without me.

3 Put the words in the right order. Write the sentences in your notebook.

1 birthday / your / really / sorry / for / I'm / forgetting

2 was / terrible / a / It / to / do / thing

3 really / I / bad / feel

4 Match the phrases with the photos.

eat cake | break tablet | not water flowers

5 Write an apology for each photo. Include an explanation with each apology.

I'm really sorry. *It was an accident.*

6 Choose one of the situations from above and write a message to apologize. (60 words)

THINK EXAMS

READING AND WRITING
Part 5: Multiple-choice cloze

1 Read the article about a strange house. Choose the best word (A, B, or C) for each space.

I **(0)**_____ on vacation with my family in California a few years **(1)** _____ when Dad saw an ad for "The Craziest House in the World." We decided to visit it, but on the way there we got lost. Dad **(2)** _____ want to ask anyone for directions, but after half an hour Mom told him to stop. We found a really **(3)** _____ man on a street in the town. He **(4)** _____ us a map, and ten minutes later we were at the house.

From the outside it just looked **(5)** _____ a normal big house. When we went inside we saw how **(6)** _____ it was. The house has 40 bedrooms, three elevators, 47 fireplaces, and 467 doors!

It was the project of a rich American woman named Sarah Winchester. They **(7)** _____ building it in 1884 and they only stopped in 1922 when Sarah died. She never drew any plans, but every time she got **(8)** _____ with the house, she just called the workers to come and build some more rooms for her.

0	A am	(B) was	C were
1	A last	B before	C ago
2	A doesn't	B did	C didn't
3	A helpful	B jealous	C confident
4	A give	B gave	C giving
5	A like	B at	C for
6	A amazed	B relaxing	C amazing
7	A start	B started	C starting
8	A bored	B boring	C interesting

Workbook page 53

Part 6: Word completion

2 Read some descriptions of furniture and words to describe people. Complete the words.

0 You usually keep your clothes in this.
   d *r e s s e r*

1 You can keep your books on this. s _ _ _ _ _

2 You use this to look at yourself. m _ _ _ _ _

3 Someone who knows a lot of things is this.
   i _ _ _ _ _ _ _ _ _ _

4 Someone who always shares their things is this.
   g _ _ _ _ _ _ _

5 Someone who is relaxed and doesn't worry much is this. e _ _ _ _ - _ _ _ _ _

Workbook page 43

Part 3: Dialogue matching

3 Complete the conversation between two friends. What does Nick say to Sue? For questions 1–5, write the correct letter A–H in each space.

SUE   It's Adam's birthday next week.
NICK **(0)** _F_
SUE   I think that's a great idea. But what?
NICK **(1)** _____
SUE   I don't think that's a good idea. He doesn't like reading.
NICK **(2)** _____
SUE   He downloads all his music. He doesn't even have a CD player.
NICK **(3)** _____
SUE   I'm not so sure. It's difficult to buy clothes for him.
NICK **(4)** _____
SUE   Let's invite him to the movies. He loves movies.
NICK **(5)** _____
SUE   Great. I'll get three tickets.

A   OK. Do you have any ideas?
B   We could get him a CD. He loves music.
C   Why don't we ask his dad?
D   Let's do that.
E   Why not?
F   ~~Why don't we get him a present?~~
G   How about buying him a book?
H   That's true. How about a T-shirt?

Workbook page 35

LISTENING
Part 2: Matching

4 ◁)) 2.02 Listen to Lauren telling Martina about her room. Who gave Lauren each of the pieces of furniture? For questions 1–5, write a letter A–H next to each present.

Present		People	
0	chair	_E_	A Dad
1	sofa	☐	B Uncle Tim
2	curtains	☐	C Aunt Abby
3	carpet	☐	D brother
4	desk	☐	E ~~Grandfather~~
5	lamp	☐	F Uncle Simon
			G Martina
			H Mom

Workbook page 61

TEST YOURSELF

VOCABULARY

1 **Use the words in the list to complete the sentences. There are two extra words.**

up | make | for | really | cheerful | do | annoying | shower | last | jealous | annoyed | stove

1 She isn't happy when I see you. I think she's a bit _____ of you.
2 I need to wash my hair, but Ian is still in the _____ .
3 Can you look _____ the address of the restaurant on your phone?
4 My sister borrowed my shoes and she didn't ask me. I was really _____ .
5 I moved to a new school and found it really difficult to _____ new friends.
6 Have you seen Anne? I'm looking _____ her.
7 He's a really _____ boy. I really don't like him.
8 I had a great time _____ night. Thanks for everything.
9 It's a _____ comfortable chair. I just want to sit in it for hours.
10 Be careful – the _____ is still hot.

/10

GRAMMAR

2 **Complete the sentences with the past form of the verbs in the list.**

buy | find | go | think | like | see

1 I _____ he was my friend, but now I'm not so sure.
2 The present was very expensive. I hope she _____ it.
3 I _____ to a party last night and got home at 11 p.m.
4 The T-shirts were on sale, so I _____ two of them.
5 We _____ a dog all alone in the street, so we took it home.
6 No, not that movie. I _____ it last week.

3 **Find and correct the mistake in each sentence.**

1 I tought you were at school. _____
2 Did you enjoyed your meal, sir? _____
3 Paul wasn't go to school today. He stayed at home. _____
4 We were tired, so we did go to bed early. _____
5 Where did you and Lucy met? _____
6 I wasn't hungry, so I didn't ate anything. _____

/12

FUNCTIONAL LANGUAGE

4 **Write the missing words.**

1 A How a_____ inviting Jake to the concert?
  B I don't think that's a good i_____ . Remember, he doesn't like crowded places.
2 A We c_____ have pizza for lunch.
  B Let's d_____ that. I love pizza!
3 A If you need some money, w_____ don't you get a part-time job?
  B I'm not so s_____ . I don't think my dad would like it.

/8

4 A L_____ go to the park after school.
  B That's a g_____ idea. We can play soccer.

MY SCORE /30

| 22 – 30 |
| 10 – 21 |
| 0 – 9 |

READING

1 🔊2.03 **What are the objects here? Match the words in the list with the photos. Write 1–6 in the boxes. Listen, check, and repeat.**

1 e-book reader | 2 camera | 3 TV
4 tablet | 5 laptop | 6 desktop computer

2 **SPEAKING** Work in pairs. Talk about the objects with a partner.

> I have a …

> I don't have a …

> I think the (laptop) in the photo looks (cool / really new / pretty old).

3 **SPEAKING** Imagine you could only have one of these things. Which would you choose?

> I'd choose the … It's important for me because … What about you?

4 🔊2.04 **Read the sentences and guess the correct answer. Listen and check your answers.**

1 A person who **invents** something *has an idea and creates something new / has enough money to buy something new.*

2 If you hear something that is **shocking**, it makes you feel *happy and excited / surprised and upset.*

3 I **researched** the topic *on the camera / on the Internet.*

4 What is a **huge** problem for Africa? *There is not enough clean water / There is not enough space for people.*

5 You can get **trachoma** from *dirty water / bad food.*

6 Getting an **eye infection** can make people *deaf / blind.*

7 You buy **gel** in a *plastic bottle / paper bag.*

5 **SPEAKING** Work in pairs. Look at the title of the article and the photos on the next page. What do you think the article is about? Compare your ideas with other students.

6 🔊2.05 **Read and listen to the article about a young inventor. Are the sentences true (T) or false (F)? Correct the false ones in your notebook.**

0 Ludwick Marishane is from South Africa. _T_

1 Ludwick used his laptop to find out more about the world's water situation. ___

2 Millions of people get trachoma every year. ___

3 Trachoma is an illness that makes people blind. ___

4 Ludwick wanted to cure people with trachoma. ___

5 DryBath doesn't help save water. ___

6 DryBath is a success. ___

7 Ludwick wants to invent more things. ___

"...just because I didn't want to take a bath"

LUDWICK MARISHANE, a 17-year-old South African, was with his friends in Limpopo when they started talking about inventing something to put on your skin so you don't have to take a bath. Ludwick thought that this was a great idea. He used his cell phone to do some research on the Internet, and he found some shocking facts.

Two point five billion people around the world don't have clean water. This is a huge problem because dirty water can create terrible illnesses. One of them is trachoma: Eight million people all over the world get trachoma every year. They wash their faces with dirty water, get an infection, and become blind. To stop trachoma, people don't have to take expensive medication. They don't have to take pills. They don't have to have injections. They just have to wash their faces with clean water. That's it.

Ludwick started thinking. He wanted to make something to help people in parts of the world where it's difficult to find clean water. He did more research on his phone, and he did more thinking. Ludwick had a plan. He wanted to make a gel for people to put on their skin so they don't have to take a bath. He wrote the formula for the gel on his phone. When he was in college, he never stopped thinking about his invention. He started to talk to other people about it, and three years later the dream came true. He made the gel and called it "DryBath."

Ludwick is the winner of lots of prizes. People call him "one of the brightest young men in the world." He is very happy about his success. DryBath is helping people to be healthy. And DryBath also helps to save water. Now Ludwick Marishane wants to invent other things, and he wants to help other young people to become inventors, too.

■ THiNK VALUES ■

Caring for people and the environment

1 **Match the values in the list with the sentences in the speech bubbles. Write a–d in the boxes.**

a caring about the environment
b caring about the quality of your work
c caring about your appearance
d caring about other people

1 *The water in a lot of rivers and lakes is not clean.* ☐

2 *I need to wash my hair. It's dirty.* ☐

3 *Are you feeling cold? I can give you my sweater.* ☐

4 *Can you turn off the radio, please? I'm doing my homework.* ☐

2 **SPEAKING Work in pairs. Ask and answer questions about Ludwick Marishane. Try and find as many answers as possible.**

Does he care about the environment?
his appearance?
the quality of his work?
other people?

Yes, because DryBath helps to save water.

GRAMMAR
have to / don't have to

1 Complete the sentences from the article on page 67 with *have to* and *don't have to*.

1 To stop trachoma, people _____ take expensive medication.

2 They _____ wash their faces with clean water.

2 Complete the rule and the table.

> RULE: Use ¹_____ to say "this is necessary."
> Use ²_____ to say "this isn't necessary."

Affirmative	Negative
I/You/We/They ⁰ __*have to*__ help.	I/You/We/They don't have to help.
He/She/It ¹_____ help.	He/She/It ²_____ help.

Questions	Short answers
³_____ I/you/we/they have to help?	Yes, I/you/we/they do. No, I/you/we/they don't.
⁴_____ he/she/it have to help?	Yes, he/she/it ⁵_____. No, he/she/it ⁶_____.

3 Match the sentences with the pictures.

1 The bus leaves in 20 minutes. He has to hurry.

2 The bus leaves in 20 minutes. He doesn't have to hurry.

4 Complete the sentences with *have to / has to* or *don't have to / doesn't have to*.

1 Our teacher doesn't like cell phones. We _____ turn them off during class.

2 I know that I _____ work hard for this test! You _____ tell me!

3 My sister is sick. She _____ stay in bed.

4 Your room is awful! You _____ clean it up.

5 Mario's English is perfect. He _____ study for the tests.

6 I can hear you very well. You _____ shout!

Workbook page 64

VOCABULARY
Gadgets

1 ◖))2.06 Match the words with the photos. Write 1–10 in the boxes. Then listen, check, and repeat.

1 GPS | 2 MP3 player | 3 flashlight | 4 game console | 5 remote control | 6 coffee maker | 7 calculator | 8 docking station | 9 hair dryer | 10 headphones |

2 How important are these gadgets for you? Give each gadget a number from 1 to 10 (1 = most important, 10 = not important at all).

3 SPEAKING Work in pairs. Compare your ideas and tell your partner how often you use these gadgets.

I often use ...   *I use my ... almost every day.*

What about you?   *I rarely use ...*

Workbook page 66

LISTENING

1 **SPEAKING** Look at the pictures of different inventions. Match them with the phrases. Write 1–4 in the boxes. Then make sentences to explain what the inventions are. Compare your ideas in class.

A ☐ **B** ☐ **C** ☐ **D** ☐

1 not clean room / have robot
2 machine help / ride bike up a hill
3 invention help homework / more time for friends
4 machine can get places around the world / 10 seconds

> The girl in picture A has a cool machine. It helps her ride her bike up a hill.

2 🔊 2.07 Martin and Anna want to become inventors. Try and match the sentence parts to find out what their situation is. Then listen and check.

1 Martin has an idea for an invention, ☐
2 He has a job, ☐
3 Anna has a lot of ideas, ☐
4 She's thirteen, ☐

a and wants to be an inventor.
b but doesn't want to say what it is.
c but doesn't know where to start.
d and doesn't have enough time to work on it.

3 🔊 2.07 Complete the expert's answers with *should* or *shouldn't*. Listen again and check.

1 You _____ start thinking "What idea can I have to make a million dollars?"
2 You _____ start with a little idea.
3 You _____ think, "What can I invent that makes one little thing in my life easier?"
4 You _____ quit your job.
5 You _____ work on your best idea first.
6 You _____ forget about your other ideas.

GRAMMAR
should / shouldn't

1 Look at the sentences in Exercise 3 of the listening. Match the sentence parts in the rule.

> **RULE:**
> 1 Use *should* to say   a "It isn't a good idea."
> 2 Use *shouldn't* to say   b "It's a good idea."

2 Use *should / shouldn't* and a word from each list to give advice to these people.

~~take~~ | go to | eat | drink | read
~~aspirin~~ | book anymore | bed
any more cake | water

0 I have a headache. *You should take an aspirin.*
1 I'm really thirsty. _____
2 My eyes are tired. _____
3 I'm tired. _____
4 I feel sick. _____

Workbook page 64 ➤

SPEAKING

Read the sentences. Decide whether you agree or disagree. Then work in pairs. Tell your partner.

1 Students shouldn't have phones in class.
2 Students should use computers in all classes.
3 There should only be six students in a classroom.
4 Students shouldn't wear school uniforms.

> I disagree with number 2. Students should use computers in most subjects but not in all of them. That would be boring.

READING

1 **SPEAKING** Work in pairs. Look at the pictures and think about what the machines do. Then choose one of the two machines and talk about it.

> I think it's called …
> It's a cool machine because …
> It helps with …
> It gets angry when …

2 Read these product reviews on a website from the year 2066. What do the robots do?

I bought the Sunny Star robot two weeks ago. It does everything for me in the morning. I don't have to do anything. It wakes me up with a nice song. I don't have to get out of bed myself. It helps me to get out of bed and carries me to the shower. Then it washes my face and brushes my teeth. It makes my bed and packs my bags for school. But you should be careful! You must not use it on rainy days. Sunny Star gets very angry when it rains. Then it only turns the cold water on when it puts you in the shower!

Do you like visiting other countries? Yes? Then Travel Plus is perfect for you. You don't have to have a lot of money. And you don't have to get up in the morning. It looks like a bed. It has a computer. You only have to type the name of a city, and it flies you there. You can stay in bed, and you can have breakfast there, too. But don't tell your teachers! They would take it away from you! Oh, and there's one more thing you should know. You must not forget to turn Travel Plus off at night. Do you know why? Because it wants to travel day and night. It waits until you're sleeping and then it starts traveling. You might wake up at the North Pole or in the middle of the ocean!

3 Read the reviews again and answer the questions.

1 What's the first thing that Sunny Star does for you in the morning?
2 When does Sunny Star create problems?
3 What does Sunny Star do when it's angry?
4 What don't you have to do when you use Travel Plus?
5 Why don't you have to get up in the morning?
6 What must you never forget to do?

GRAMMAR
must not / don't have to

1 Complete the sentences from the reviews. Then complete the rule with *must not* or *don't have to*.

1 You _____ do anything. Sunny Star does all the work for you.
2 You _____ forget to turn Travel Plus off at night.

> RULE: Use ¹_____ to say "it isn't necessary."
> Use ²_____ to say "don't do it! I'm telling you not to!"

2 Match sentences 1–2 with a–b.

1 You don't have to go swimming. _____
2 You must not go swimming. _____

a There are sharks.
b You can do something else if you prefer.

3 Complete the sentences with *must not* or *don't have to*.

1 A Dad, I don't want to go to the park with you.
  B No problem. You _____ be there.
2 A I'm almost ready, Mom.
  B Hurry! You _____ be late for class again!
3 A I'm sorry I can't join you.
  B That's fine. You _____ come.
4 A Sorry, I can't stay. I'm in a hurry.
  B Oh, no problem. You _____ wait for me.
5 A I don't like swimming.
  B We _____ go swimming. We can go to the park.
6 A You _____ leave the gate open. The dog can get out.
  B Oh, right. I forgot. Sorry.

Workbook page 65

Pronunciation
Vowel sounds: /ʊ/ and /u/
Go to page 121.

VOCABULARY
Housework

🔊 2.10 Match the words with the photos. Write 1–10 in the boxes. Listen and check. Then listen again and repeat.

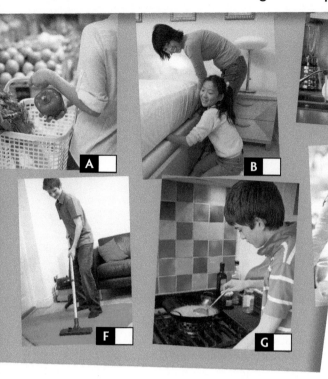

1 vacuum | 2 clean | 3 do the ironing
4 buy groceries | 5 set / clear the table
6 do/wash the dishes | 7 make the beds
8 cook | 9 do laundry
10 load / empty the dishwasher

Workbook page 66

SPEAKING

1 **Read the questions. Make notes.**

1 What types of housework do you have to do at home?
2 What don't you have to do?
3 What jobs around the house should parents / children do?

2 **Plan what you are going to say. Use these phrases.**

> I have to ... I think / don't think that's fair.

> I don't have to ... I'm pretty happy about that.
> But it would be OK for me to do that.

> I think ... should do the same amount of work.
> It's not fair that ...
> Parents should do more work because ...

3 **Work in pairs or small groups. Compare your ideas about housework.**

WRITING
A paragraph about housework

Ask your partner these questions and take notes. Then write a paragraph in your notebook.

1 What do you have to do at home?
2 What don't you have to do at home?
3 When do you have to do housework?
4 How do you feel about this housework?

Kate hates clearing the table, but she has to do it every evening. She also has to vacuum her bedroom once a week. She doesn't have to do ...

■ THiNK SELF-ESTEEM ■
Classroom rules

1 **Write sentences about things students *have to*, *should(n't)*, or *must not* do.**
Students have to study for their tests.
Students should speak English as much as possible.
Students must not eat during class.

2 **SPEAKING Compare your sentences in class. Say what you think.**

> I think it's a good idea / fair / not fair that ...

> I think students / teachers / we all should(n't) ...

3 **Vote on a set of rules for your class. Make a poster, sign it, and put it on the wall.**

The treasure hunt

1 🔊 2.11 **Read and listen to the photostory and answer the questions.**

Why can't Ryan come to Luke's house after school?
What's a GPS treasure hunt?

LUKE Hey, come to my house later?
RYAN Sorry, no way. I have things to do.
LUKE Oh, yeah? Like what, Ryan?
RYAN Oh, homework and stuff. And I promised to help my dad. Sorry.
LUKE OK. Never mind.

1

RYAN Hey, come here, Luke. I've found something. It looks like a box. It IS a box!
LUKE What's in it? Gold coins? Diamonds? "Ladies and gentlemen. We are now talking live to the two lucky boys who found the treasure in the park."
RYAN Very funny.
LUKE Yeah, yeah. Come on, open the box!

2

RYAN What do we do now?
LUKE Eat it?
RYAN That sounds like a good idea. But hurry up.
LUKE What do you mean?
RYAN Look. Olivia and Megan are coming. I don't want to share it with them.

3

LUKE Hi, you two.
RYAN So, what are you up to? Using the GPS on your phone to find your way home?
MEGAN No. We're on a treasure hunt.
RYAN What?
MEGAN We're trying to find some treasure. Here in the park. Using the GPS on my phone. It's so much fun!
LUKE Treasure? You mean, like a box with a little surprise in it?
OLIVIA Exactly! Now, can we keep looking?

4

DEVELOPING SPEAKING

2 Work in pairs. Discuss what happens next in the story. Write down your ideas.

We think Olivia and Megan find the box. They find … there.

3 ▶ **EP4** Watch to find out how the story continues.

4 Answer the questions.

1 What is Luke worried about?
2 Where does Ryan think Luke is going?
3 What's the problem with the phone?
4 What does Olivia do to solve the problem?
5 What's the problem for Luke and Ryan?
6 What do the girls find in the box?

PHRASES FOR FLUENCY

1 Find the expressions 1–5 in the story. Who says them? How do you say them in your language?

0 Sorry, no way.   *Ryan*
1 … and stuff.   _____
2 Never mind.   _____
3 Yeah, yeah.   _____
4 So, … ?   _____
5 … so much fun.   _____

2 Complete the dialogue with the expressions in Exercise 1.

A Do you want to come over tonight? We can play games on the computer [1]_____ .

B Sure! Computer games are [2]_____ .

A Hey, can you bring your new laptop?

B [3]_____ . It's my brother's, too. I can't take it.

A [4]_____ . We can use mine, since you're afraid of your little brother.

B [5]_____ , I'm so afraid of him. [6]_____ , seven o'clock then?

WordWise
Expressions with *like*

1 Complete the sentences from the story with the phrases in the list.

like | looks like | sounds like | Like what

1 Oh, yeah? _____ , Ryan?
2 It _____ a box. It IS a box.
3 That _____ a good idea.
4 Treasure? You mean, _____ a box with a little surprise in it?

2 Match the sentences.

1 This chicken isn't very good.
2 Someone's talking. Who is it?
3 Let's buy her a present.
4 He's a really nice guy.
5 What's that animal?

a Like what? A poster?
b Yes, he's just like his sister. She's nice, too.
c I'm not sure. It looks like a dog, but it isn't.
d That's right. It tastes like fish!
e It sounds like Jim.

3 Complete the dialogues using a phrase with *like*.

1 **A** I really hate tomatoes.
  B I'm _____ you. I hate them, too.
2 **A** Here's a photo of my sister.
  B Wow. She really _____ you!
3 **A** I'm bored. We should do something.
  B _____ ? Go for a walk?
4 **A** Let's go to the movies.
  B That _____ a great idea.

▶ Workbook page 66

FUNCTIONS
Asking for repetition and clarification

1 Complete the extracts from the conversations with the words from the list.

you mean | What? | Like what

LUKE	Hey, come to my house later?
RYAN	Sorry, no way. I have things to do.
LUKE	[1]_____ , Ryan?
RYAN	That sounds like a good idea. But hurry up!
LUKE	What do [2]_____ ?
MEGAN	We're on a treasure hunt.
RYAN	[3]_____
MEGAN	We're trying to find some treasure.

2 Match the expressions in Exercise 1 with their definitions.

a Say that again.
b What are you trying to say?
c Give me an example.

ROLE PLAY A phone call

Work in pairs. Student A: Go to page 127. Student B: Go to page 128. Take two or three minutes to prepare. Then have a conversation.

8 | FREE TIME

A

B

C

D

E

F

READING

1 Look at the photos. Use words in the list to say why the people need help or how they are helping.

clean up | disabled | a flood | home
a mural | raise money | sick | trash

	man		has no… / is …
The	woman	in picture …	is…ing …
	children		have no… / are…
	people		are …ing …

2 What charities do you know about in your country? How do they help?

> *The World Wildlife Fund helps protect animals and the environment.*

3 A volunteer is a person who works but doesn't get paid for their work. Look at the article on the next page for one minute and answer the questions.

1 How old is the girl in the photo?
2 What does she like most about her work?
3 What's the name of the charity?
4 What does the charity do?

4 **SPEAKING** Compare your answers with a partner.

5 ◁〉2.12 Read and listen to the article again. Correct the information in these sentences.

1 Right now, Mary is preparing beds for the guests.

_____

2 Mary works for Teen Feed three mornings a week.

_____

3 Mary works in only one of Teen Feed's locations.

_____

4 Mary says that the teens all have the same story.

_____

5 Mary doesn't like the other volunteers very much.

_____

6 Mary doesn't ever like to waste time.

_____

MARY GIVES EVERYTHING FOR TEEN FEED!

Mary Kapitonenko gives up some of her free time each week to work at Teen Feed and help teenagers in need. Mary's only 16 years old – she is friends with many of the kids in the program – but she works as hard as the adult volunteers. Mary is thoughtful, funny, and a great artist. We at Teen Feed are so happy she is one of our volunteers.

We are pleased to name Mary Kapitonenko **September's Volunteer of the Month!**

So, Mary, what are you doing right now?
I'm helping in the kitchen. We're preparing food for our guests in the Teen Feed program. They are teenagers who have no home and who are hungry.

Why are you a volunteer for Teen Feed?
My friend told me about Teen Feed last year. I really liked the idea of helping people in need, so I started volunteering on Saturdays in the University District. Now I also go to the program in another part of the city. So I help on Thursday, Friday, and Saturday nights.

That's a lot of work. How were you last night, after coming home?
Very happy! But also very tired.

What do you like most about Teen Feed?
The thing I like most about volunteering is that I can help teenagers. Some people think it's the young people's fault that they have no food. They think these teens are bad, but that's not true. I like talking to our guests. I'm really interested in them. They all have interesting stories to share. And of course, I like the other volunteers at Teen Feed.

What do you do outside of Teen Feed?
I hang out with my friends, I draw, and I like being lazy sometimes.

What did you eat today?
Coffee, a chocolate protein shake, a peanut butter and banana sandwich, and a glass of milk.

Thank you so much for ALL you do, Mary!
To learn more about Teen Feed, click here. To support Teen Feed's work, click here.

■ THiNK VALUES ■

Giving your time to others

1 **Read what people say about the Teen Feed program.**

> *It's all those teenagers' fault. They should get a job.*

> *The volunteers give so much time and energy to people they don't know. I could never do that.*

> *I often give money to people who need it. That's more important than volunteering.*

> *A young volunteer can learn a lot from helping other people.*

2 **SPEAKING** Work with a partner. Imagine you are Mary. Write your ideas about the statements in Exercise 1. Read them to the class and talk about them.

GRAMMAR
Review of question forms

1 **Use the article on page 75 to complete the questions.**

1 What _____ you _____ right now?
(_____ *present continuous* _____)

2 Why _____ you a volunteer for Teen Feed?
(_____)

3 How _____ you last night, after coming home?
(_____)

4 What _____ you _____ most about Teen Feed? (_____)

5 What _____ you _____ today?
(_____)

2 **Write *simple past (be)*, *simple past*, *simple present (be)*, *simple present*, or *present continuous* for the questions in Exercise 1.**

3 **Complete the rules with the words in the list.**

do / does | ~~*question word*~~ | *verb + ing*
did | *was / were*

> **RULE:** To form a question
> - in the simple present (*be*), use [0] *question word* + form of *be*.
> - in the simple present, use question word + [1] _____ + the verb.
> - in the present continuous, use question word + form of *be* + [2] _____ .
> - in the simple past, use question word + [3] _____ + verb.
> - in the simple past (*be*), use question word + [4] _____ .

4 **Put the words in the correct order to make the questions.**

1 you / what / doing / are / ?
_____

2 you / where / Sunday / last / were / ?
_____

3 best / your / friends / who / are / two / ?
_____

4 you / this / eat / what / did / for breakfast / morning / ?
_____

5 get up / do / on weekends / you / when / ?
_____

6 were /on vacation / how long / you / ?
_____

5 **With a partner, ask and answer the questions in Exercise 4.**

> **Pronunciation**
> Stress in numbers
> Go to page 121. 🔊

Workbook page 72 ▶

VOCABULARY
Collocations with *time*

1 🔊 **2.15 Read the sentences. Circle the correct word. Then listen and check.**

1 Mary Kapitonenko *spends* / *brings* a lot of time helping other people.

2 Don't *waste* / *lose* your time. You have a lot of homework to do.

3 I never *keep* / *find* time to relax and read a book.

4 We *had* / *took* a great time at Sandra's birthday party.

5 I'm sorry to hear you're *having* / *spending* such a bad time.

6 She loves painting in her *extra* / *spare* time.

7 He's so busy. He can never take time *away* / *off*.

2 **Write the questions.**

0 often / waste time / ?
Do you often waste time?

1 when / last / have / great time / ?
_____

2 how / spend your time / last Sunday / ?
_____

3 have a good time / now / ?
_____

4 why / so difficult / take time off / ?
_____

5 find time / to see / your friends / ?
_____

3 **SPEAKING With a partner, ask and answer the questions from Exercise 2.**

Workbook page 74 ▶

LISTENING

1 ◀》2.16 **Listen to the interviews and write the names under the pictures.**

1 _____

2 _____

3 _____

4 _____

2 ◀》2.16 **Listen again and answer the questions.**

1 What does Dylan do on weekends?
_____

2 How does he feel he wastes time?
_____

3 What does Daisy do on Sundays?
_____

4 What does she do Saturday nights?
_____

5 What does Josh do on Sundays?
_____

6 Does he think he wastes time? Why or why not?
_____

7 What does Chloe do on Saturdays?
_____

8 What does Chloe do on Sundays?
_____

3 SPEAKING **Work with a partner. Who are you most like, and why?**

> I'm most like Daisy because I play a lot of sports on the weekend.

■ TRAIN TO THiNK ■

Creative thinking

1 WRITING **Imagine people don't have to sleep anymore. Think about the questions and write as many sentences as you can in your notebook.**

1 How does the world change as a result?
People have more … / can … / can't …
Everybody is … / can … / wants to …
Nobody is … / can … / wants to …
Stores …

2 How does your life change?
With the extra time, I can … /
My parents …
My best friends …

2 **Read your ideas to each other in a small group. Are they the same or different?**

READING

1 Read the messages. Which of Matt's suggestions does Jake take?

Hey Matt – I need help! I'm stuck at the Paris airport with my family. The plane's delayed for four hours. That's right. Four hours!!! [1] Any ideas what I can do to kill time? Help me, please!

Sorry to hear that, Jake. What's the airport like? Are there any stores? I'm sure there are. Go and buy me a present. That's a good way to waste half an hour.

That was the first thing I did – check the airport out, not buy you a present! It's big. There are some little stores, nothing too exciting. I'm tired of looking at handbags and perfume. [2] Any other ideas?

OK, so you don't want to go shopping. Why don't you watch a movie on your phone?

I hate watching movies on my phone. The screen's too small. Besides, I watched one on the flight here. The new X-Men movie.

I really want to see that. What was it like? Any good? [3]

It's was good. Really exciting. But you know me – love superhero movies! It's too bad they all die. [4] I'm still bored!!! I need some more ideas. NOW!

Listen to some music. Eat something. Talk to your sister. Read a book. Count how many windows there are in the airport. Are these any good?

My headphones are broken. I'm not hungry. Are you kidding? I don't have a book. I can see 56 windows. No, none of these ideas is any good.

OK, one last suggestion. I have a life too, you know. Go and talk to a local. Practice some of that French we learned last year.

Well, there is a girl sitting across from me. And she's smiling at me. [5] Maybe that's not such a bad idea. TTYL.

Yeah? What's she like?

Hey Jake. What's she like?

Are you still there? Answer me.

Jake, answer me!

2 Read the messages again. Where do these missing pieces of information come from? Write 1–5.

	a I think she's French.
	b My mom isn't, though.
	c It's our very first vacation abroad.
	d But don't tell me the end!
	e Just joking.

3 SPEAKING Discuss in pairs. Imagine your friend is home sick and really bored. He or she texts you for suggestions about what to do. Make a list of four things. Then compare your list with another pair's list.

GRAMMAR
What + be + like?

1 **Match the questions to the answers. Then complete the rule. Use the same word in both places.**

1 What's the airport like? _____	a It was good. Really exciting.
2 What was the movie like? _____	b She's very pretty and a lot of fun.
3 What's she like? _____	c It's big, and there are some little stores.

RULE: To ask about the qualities of something, we can use *What + be +* ¹_____ ?

The answer is usually an adjective or a short descriptive phrase. We don't use ²_____ in the answer.

2 **Write questions to find out more about these statements.**

1 A I went to Canada on vacation.
   B Really? *What was it like?*

2 A We have a new English teacher named Mr. French!
   B That's a funny name for an English teacher.
   _____?

3 A Try this new game. I think you'll like it.
   B Why? _____?

4 A Try one of these little pies.
   B I don't know. They look strange.
   _____?

5 A If you're going out, put on a coat.
   B Why? _____?

6 A I went to Julia's party on Saturday.
   B _____?

3 **Now match these answers to the questions you wrote in Exercise 2. Write 1–6.**

a ☐ They're delicious. They're really sweet.
b ☐ It's similar to Warrior Planet, but with better graphics.
c ☐ It was fun. I danced a lot.
d ☐ It was great. It's a really beautiful country.
e ☐ He's sort of serious, but he's a really good teacher.
f ☐ It's windy and cold.

Workbook page 73

VOCABULARY
Descriptive adjectives

1 **Work with a partner. Think of three adjectives you could use to answer the questions.**

1 What's this movie like?
   exciting
   _____
   _____

2 What's she like?
   _____
   _____
   _____

3 What's the cake like?
   _____
   _____
   _____

4 What was London like?
   _____
   _____
   _____

2 **Which of these adjectives can answer the questions in Exercise 1? Use a dictionary to help you.**

crowded | light | chocolaty | action-packed
arrogant | dirty | dull | thoughtful

3 **On four separate pieces of paper, write the information. Give the pieces to a partner.**

1 the last movie I saw
2 the last place I went on vacation
3 the name of a friend
4 a meal my family often has on special days

4 **SPEAKING Ask about the things that your partner wrote.**

Sukiyaki – what's that?

It's a Japanese dish my dad makes when my grandparents visit.

What's it like?   Really delicious!

Workbook page 74

79

Culture

1 **Look at the photos. Where can you see these things? More than one answer is possible.**

1 a volunteer in a hospital
2 someone working on a farm
3 someone teaching little kids
4 someone working with wild animals
5 someone planting trees
6 someone building a school

 A
 B
 C
 D
 E
 F

2 **Which type of volunteer work interests you the most? Why?**

3 🔊 2.17 **Read and listen to the article. Match the photos to the different organizations.**

VOLUNTEERING ABROAD

So, you're interested in volunteering abroad, but you're not sure what you want to do, where you want to go, or how long you want to be a volunteer. There are a large number of organizations that offer people different kinds of volunteer projects around the world. These sites can help you choose the one that's right for you.

1 One World 365 _____

If you are considering traveling somewhere in the world, you can find out about opportunities to do volunteer work at the same time as you travel. This website has information about hundreds of meaningful volunteer programs all over the world. You could volunteer with elephants in Sri Lanka, help environmental projects in South Africa, help community development projects in Tanzania, work with orphans and other children in need in Romania, or protect conservation areas and animals in the Amazon. Go to their website to check out all the possibilities.

2 WWOOF _____

Want to get your hands dirty? WWOOF stands for World Wide Opportunities on Organic Farms. Its goal is to help people who would like to get involved with organic farming in different countries around the world. In your chosen country, you live with a family. You get a bed and food in exchange for four to six hours of work a day on their farm. What you do depends on the farm, of course, but it can include milking animals, planting trees or vegetables, cutting wood, or one of a thousand other things. Usually people stay on the farm for a few weeks, but it's possible to stay for as long as six months.

3 Global Volunteers _____

Like most of the other organizations listed here, Global Volunteers is a non-profit. It helps people of all ages to go to another country and work with people who need help. You could, for example, go to Africa and work in a school – either teaching or helping to build or repair school buildings. But unlike some other volunteer organizations, Global Volunteers welcomes people of all ages. Some of their volunteers are as old as 55. But these days there are more and more young people, even some under 21, who are getting involved.

Why volunteer abroad? Here's what one volunteer said:

"I get so much more than I give. Volunteering like this gives you insight into the culture in a way you could never get as a tourist. You live with the people, you go to their homes, and mix with teachers. You realize you have something in common with the people you're working with."

4 **Read the article again and answer the questions.**

1 Are these the only volunteer organizations on the Web?

2 What do volunteers on farms get if they agree to work for four to six hours a day?

3 How long do volunteers normally stay on a farm?

4 What could you do in a school in Tanzania?

5 What does one volunteer think you learn from mixing with people in a different culture?

5 **VOCABULARY** **There are eight highlighted words or phrases in the article. Match them with these meanings. Write the words.**

0 to share interests or experience *have something in common*

1 becoming part of an important experience _____

2 a clear, deep understanding of a situation _____

3 thinking about _____

4 given because you have given something _____

5 important or useful _____

6 getting milk from cows, goats, etc. _____

7 children who don't have parents _____

WRITING
A volunteer's blog

1 **Read Victoria's blog entry about her volunteer experience. Number the photographs in the order she talks about them.**

2 **Read the blog entry again. Who or what is/was:**

1 delicious _____

2 easy _____

3 exhausted _____

4 fun _____

5 rewarding _____

3 **Imagine that you are one of these volunteers and then answer the questions. Use your imagination and the ideas in Victoria's blog.**

- someone working with sick and injured elephants in Asia
- someone working with sick children in a hospital in a poor country
- someone helping to teach children in a school in a poor area of the city
- someone helping to clean up after a natural disaster, like a flood or an earthquake

1 What time do you get up in the morning?

2 What time do you have breakfast / lunch / dinner?

3 What do you do in the mornings?

4 What do you do in the afternoons?

5 What time do you go to bed? How do you feel then?

4 **Write a blog entry as the volunteer. Use your answers to the questions in Exercise 3 to help you. Use some of the vocabulary from the Culture section on page 80. Write 120–150 words.**

Monday, April 21

Today we woke up very early – 5:30. It was a little cold and it was still dark, but everyone was happy after sleeping for eight hours! We went into the kitchen and had a delicious breakfast – fruit and some coffee, and a piece of fresh bread.

Then I went to milk the cows. The first time I did this was a week ago. I didn't know how to do it, but now it's easy. Then I went with the others to the fields. The corn is ready to harvest now, so from seven o'clock until noon, we worked in the fields cutting the corn. It smells so good! There are six of us and the fields are very big, so we were all exhausted when we stopped for lunch. Hungry, too!

After lunch, some of the volunteers worked in the fields more. Others, including me, went to the local school. Some of us teach English there. Today we sang some songs with the kids and then we played a game to help them learn the names of colors. That was so much fun, and the kids did really well. Teaching is very rewarding!

Now it's nine o'clock and I'm in bed already. I'm always really tired at the end of the day. And guess what we had for dinner tonight – corn! Yum.

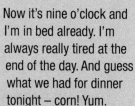

CAMBRIDGE ENGLISH: Key

▌THiNK EXAMS

READING AND WRITING
Part 1: Matching
Workbook page 71 ▶

1 Which notice (A–H) says this (1–5)? Write the letters A–H.

0	Adults only.	C
1	You don't have to pay if you're eight.	
2	You shouldn't leave your car here.	
3	The store is closed in the afternoon.	
4	You should call for more information.	
5	You must not swim here.	

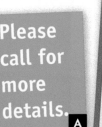

Please call for more details. **A**

• Museum • FREE to children under nine **B**

You have to be over 18 to watch this movie. **C**

Please DON'T park in front of our store. **D**

STORE HOURS 9 – 11:30 a.m. **E**

DANGEROUS DEEP WATER KEEP OUT **F**

CLOSED on Saturdays **G**

Parking $2 per hour **H**

Part 3: Multiple-choice replies
Workbook page 17 ▶

2 Complete five conversations. Choose the correct answer A, B, or C.

0 It's not cold today.
- A You must not wear shorts.
- B You must wear a jacket.
- (C) You don't have to wear a sweater.

1 It's very dark. I can't see anything.
- A You need some headphones.
- B Here's a flashlight for you.
- C I have a docking station, if you want.

2 I have a headache.
- A You should go to bed for half an hour.
- B You should watch TV.
- C You shouldn't get some rest.

3 What's Isabel like?
- A Yes, I like her a lot.
- B She likes pizza and baseball.
- C She's smart and very funny.

4 What is your dad doing?
- A He's a doctor at City Hospital.
- B He walks in the park every morning.
- C He's practicing the piano.

5 Do you want to go to the movies?
- A No, I have to.
- B Sorry. I have to clean my room.
- C Yes, I must.

LISTENING
Part 4: Note taking
Workbook page 79 ▶

3 ◀》2.18 You will hear an interview with a famous person. Listen and complete 1–5.

Interview

Name:	0	_Joe Ruby_
Age:	1	
Product:	2	
Company name:	3	
Price:	4	
Vacation destination:	5	

TEST YOURSELF

VOCABULARY

1 **Complete the sentences with the words in the list. There are two extra words.**

calculator | arrogant | remote control | coffee maker | does | headphones
waste | dishes | thoughtful | GPS | make | spend

1 We're lost. Do you have _____ on your phone?
2 I have to _____ my bed every morning before I go to school.
3 What a mess – next time, we should wash the _____ right after dinner.
4 She's so _____ . She thinks she's better than everyone!
5 What is 7% of 270? I need a _____ .
6 Don't _____ time on video games. The test is tomorrow!
7 Pass me the _____ , please. I want to watch the news.
8 Her grades aren't good. She needs to _____ more time on her homework.
9 Dad _____ the laundry in my house.
10 I'm trying to work, and your music is too loud. Can you wear _____ ?

/10

GRAMMAR

2 **Complete the questions with the correct form of *be* or *do*.**

1 What show _____ you watching? It looks very interesting.
2 Sarah wasn't in class yesterday. Where _____ she?
3 What time _____ you usually go to bed on the weekend?
4 Where _____ you buy those headphones? They look cool!
5 Where _____ you? It's 7:30, and I'm waiting in front of the theater.
6 Why _____ your dad using GPS? He drives around here all the time.

3 **Find and correct the mistake in each sentence.**

1 Where did you went yesterday?   _____
2 You not have to go if you don't want to.   _____
3 We must not run. The train doesn't go for an hour. _____
4 You must to be careful. It's very dangerous.   _____
5 How are they get to school every morning?   _____
6 What's he like? Well, he's like very quiet and serious. _____

/12

FUNCTIONAL LANGUAGE

4 **Write the missing words.**

1 A You _____ have to eat it if you don't want to.
  B Thanks, I don't _____ like it.
2 A I can't come to your house. I have lots of things to do.
  B Like _____ ?
  A Well, I have to help my dad _____ the laundry, for a start.
3 A Thank you so _____ for all of your _____ .
4 A I went to Rob's party _____ weekend.
  B Really? What was it _____ ?
  A Pretty boring, actually.

/8

MY SCORE [   ] /30

| 22 – 30 |
| 10 – 21 |
| 0 – 9 |

OBJECTIVES

FUNCTIONS: paying compliments; talking about the weather

GRAMMAR: comparative adjectives; *can / can't* for ability; superlative adjectives

VOCABULARY: geographical features; the weather; phrases with *with*

An amazing place

They eat wild animals, plants, berries, nuts, and insects. They hunt with bows and arrows. There are lots of dangerous snakes, spiders, and scorpions. There are lions, leopards, cheetahs, and hyenas. It's one of southern Africa's hottest places, and there is often no water. Then they have to get their water from plants, for example, from desert melons. When they are sick, there are no hospitals. The people have to get their medicine from plants, too.

They are the San, the last people living in the Kalahari. The San people have another name – "bush people." Their lifestyle is very simple, but they know more about animals and plants than most people do. The San people live in small groups of twenty-five to fifty. They live in huts – little houses that they make from wood and grass. There are no schools for the children. Children learn from the older people in the group. There are lots of things they have to learn so that they can live in a dangerous place like the Kalahari. In the evenings, the groups of people often sit around a fire and tell stories. Many of the stories are about animals and how to hunt them.

The Kalahari is a big area of bushland in southern Africa. It has two parts. There is less rain in the southern part than there is in the northern part, so the south is drier. There are fewer plants and animals there, and it's a lot more difficult for people to live. But when it rains at the end of the summer, the land becomes greener and more beautiful. For a few weeks, there are millions of little flowers and even butterflies!

READING

1 Look at the photos. Which of the animals can you name in English?

2 Name other animals in English. Write them down.

3 [SPEAKING] Work in pairs. Look at the animals on your list. What countries do you think of?

> Pandas come from China.

> You find spiders all over the world.

4 [SPEAKING] Work in pairs. Look at the photos again and answer the questions.

1 What do the photos show?
2 Where do these people live?
3 What do you think they eat?
4 What dangers are there in this place?
5 What do these people know a lot about?
6 What's interesting for tourists about this place?

5 🔊 2.19 Read and listen to the article. Mark the statements T (True) or F (False). Correct the false information in your notebook.

1 The bush people always get their water from plants. _____
2 When the San people are sick, they get medicine from a hospital. _____
3 The bush people teach children important things about living in the Kalahari. _____
4 The north of the Kalahari is wetter than the south. _____
5 Many San people today work with tourists. _____
6 A vacation in the Kalahari is never dangerous. _____

But soon, the grass and the bushes get dry and turn brown. Then life becomes more difficult again for people and animals.

Every year, thousands of tourists from all over the world visit the Kalahari. They love driving around the bushland in open jeeps. They love watching the wild animals. Their guides are often San Bushmen, and the tourists love listening to their stories about the wonders of the Kalahari. The tourists stay in small huts called "lodges." They have comfortable beds and showers, but there is no electricity in the huts. When they go out of their hut, they have to be very careful. Sometimes there are lions or leopards around!

6 SPEAKING **Work in pairs or small groups and answer these questions.**

1 Would you like to go to the Kalahari? Why or why not?

2 What wildlife are you interested in?

> I'd love to / I wouldn't like to … because …

> I'm (not) interested in …

> I think it's too dangerous to … / wonderful to …

> I love / hate taking photos.
> watching … / staying in …

■ THiNK VALUES ■

Valuing our world

1 **Read and check (✓) the statements that show that the natural world is important.**

1 Why should I want to go on a safari? There's a nice zoo in my city where I can see lots of animals. ☐

2 I want to build a hotel for 800 people in the Kalahari Desert. We can make a lot of money like that. ☐

3 It's great to learn about wild animals. It helps me to understand more about the world. ☐

4 Who needs lions, leopards, and hyenas? They're dangerous animals! ☐

5 I watch a lot of nature shows on TV. I support a project to save tigers in India. ☐

2 SPEAKING **Compare your ideas in pairs.**

> Statement 1 shows that the natural world is not important for this person.

> Why do you think that?

> Because the person doesn't want to see wild animals in nature.

> But maybe that's not true. Maybe he or she thinks flying to other places is not good for nature.

GRAMMAR
Comparative adjectives

1 Look at the article on page 84 again. Find examples of comparisons. Then complete the table on the right.

2 Complete the sentences. Use the comparative form of the adjectives.

1 Africa is _____ (big) than South America, but _____ (small) than Asia.

2 Be careful of the spiders in the Kalahari. They're _____ (dangerous) than the ones at home.

3 Cars these days are _____ (good) quality than they were 30 years ago.

4 For me, vacations in the Kalahari are _____ (interesting) than going to the beach.

5 My sister has two children. Her son is nine. His sister is two years _____ (young).

6 John is a musician. It's _____ (easy) for him to learn a new instrument than it is for me.

	adjectives	comparative form
short adjectives (one syllable)	small	0 _smaller_ (than)
	big	bigger (than)
	hot	1 _____ (than)
adjectives ending in consonant + -y	happy	happier (than)
	dry	2 _____ (than)
	early	3 _____ (than)
longer adjectives (two or more syllables)	attractive	4 _____ (than)
	beautiful	more beautiful (than)
irregular adjectives	bad	worse (than)
	good	5 _____ (than)
	far	farther / further (than)

Workbook page 82

VOCABULARY
Geographical features

1 🔊2.20 Label the picture with the words. Write 1–12 in the boxes. Then listen, check, and repeat.

1 ocean | 2 hill | 3 mountain | 4 jungle | 5 river | 6 desert | 7 lake | 8 beach | 9 island | 10 forest

2 SPEAKING Work in pairs. Ask your partner to close their book and then ask them about the picture.

What's A?

I think it's … / I'm not sure if I can remember. Is it … ? / Can you give me the first letter, please?

3 SPEAKING Work in pairs. Compare some of the places. Use the adjectives in the list to help you or use other adjectives.

hot | big | dangerous | high | nice difficult | beautiful | exciting

A mountain is higher than a hill.

Yes, and it's more difficult to climb a mountain.

Workbook page 84

LISTENING

1 **Match the things in the list with the photos. Write 1–4 in the boxes.**

1 vultures | 2 a lion and its kill | 3 a spear | 4 an antelope

2 🔊2.21 **Listen to an interview with a Bushman from the Kalahari. Check (✓) the title that best sums up what he talks about.**

1 Life in the Kalahari
2 Lions, vultures, and antelopes
3 A difficult task for a young man
4 Big cats of Africa

3 🔊2.21 **Listen again. For questions 1–5, check (✓) A, B, or C.**

1 Where was PK born?
A in the Kalahari
B in the Sahara
C in Kenya

2 Before a young man can get married, he has to
A do a task.
B find a lion.
C kill an antelope.

3 It's important for the future family that the young man
A kills many lions.
B likes the girl's father.
C has courage.

4 What can show the Bushman where the lion is eating?
A antelopes
B vultures
C his future family

5 To take the kill away from the lion, you have to
A run faster than the lion can.
B attack the lion with your spear.
C be very quiet and surprise the lion.

GRAMMAR
can / can't for ability

1 **Look at the examples. How do you say these sentences in your language?**

1 A man **can** run even when it's very hot.
2 Lions **can't** do that.

2 **Look at these sentences from the interview. Complete them with can or can't.**

1 How _____ you find a lion and its kill?
2 You _____ get the kill from the lion at night.
3 How _____ you take the meat away from the lion?

3 **Complete the table.**

Affirmative	I/You/We/They/He/She/It **can** run fast.
Negative	I/You/We/They/He/She/It ¹_____ (**cannot**) run fast.
Questions	²_____ I/you/we/they/he/she/it run fast?
Short answers	Yes, I/you/we/they/he/she/it **can**. No, I/you/we/they/he/she/it ³_____ (**cannot**).

4 **Make sentences with can and can't.**

0 Simon + run fast / – swim fast
   Simon can run fast, but he can't swim fast.
1 Matt + drive a car / – fly a plane
   Matt _____
2 Dogs + understand humans / – speak
   Dogs _____
3 I + write emails / – do math on my laptop
   I _____
4 They + write good songs / – sing well
   They _____

Workbook page 82

■ THiNK SELF-ESTEEM
Being brave

SPEAKING **Think about and answer these questions. Compare your ideas with a partner.**

1 In what situations do people have to show courage?
2 When is it difficult to show courage?
3 Who could be a role model for you in situations where you need to show courage?

People have to show courage when they are in new situations.

It's difficult to show courage when you're scared.

READING

1 Read the article. Where's the world's driest place?

Could you live there?

Death Valley, California

Italy

Antarctica

1 The hottest place on Earth
Death Valley is one of the world's hottest areas, but the place with the record for the highest temperature is El Aziziya in Libya. There, the temperature reached a record of 57.8°C in 1922. Death Valley's highest temperature on record is 56.7°C. That's not a lot cooler!

2 Antarctica – extreme weather records
Antarctica is the most fascinating place for extreme weather. It's the world's coldest place. And it's the wettest but also the driest place. Are you surprised? Well, here are the facts. People cannot live in Antarctica all year round because it's too cold. In 1983 scientists recorded the lowest temperature ever: -89.4°C! It's also the wettest place on earth, but not because of rain or snow. It's the wettest place because 98% of Antarctica is covered in ice. But it's also the driest place because it never rains there – it only snows! Antarctica holds another record, too. One area has the world's thickest ice: it's 2,555 meters deep!

3 The world's best and worst weather
So, where are the best and worst places in the world for weather? That's a difficult question. What's good for one person may be bad for another. In 2012 an organization called International Living came up with a list. Their number 1 for the best weather was Italy, their number 2 was France, and Mexico was number 3! Where do you think your country would rank?

2 Read the article again. Answer the questions.

1 Which is hotter, El Aziziya or Death Valley?
2 What place is the wettest place on earth?
3 Why is it difficult to say where the world's best and worst weather is?

SPEAKING

Work in pairs. Discuss these questions.

1 Which of the facts did you know before?
2 Which of the facts were new to you?
3 Which of the places mentioned would you like to visit most? Why?
4 What's your answer to the question at the end of the article? Give your reasons.

Pronunciation

Vowel sounds: /ɪ/ and /aɪ/

Go to page 121.

WRITING

An email about a place

Imagine you want to tell a friend about the place in the article that you find most interesting. Write an email (100–125 words) in your notebook.

- Choose the place.
- In your email, say
  – where the place is.
  – what's special about the weather there.
  – why you think it's interesting.

GRAMMAR

Superlative adjectives

1 Put the words in order to make sentences. Check your answers in the article.

1 world's / hottest / is / of / Death Valley / the / places / one
2 for / the / is / most fascinating / Antarctica / extreme / place / weather
3 coldest / the / place / world's / It's
4 the / Where / weather? / are / and / best / for / worst / places

2 **Look at the table. Complete the "adjectives" column with the words in the list. Then write the comparative and superlative forms.**

~~low~~ | fascinating | happy | bad | hot

	adjectives	comparative form	superlative form
short adjectives (one syllable)	0 _low_ high thick	lower 5 _____ 6 _____	the lowest 14 _____ 15 _____
short adjectives ending in one vowel + one consonant	1 _____ wet	hotter 7 _____	16 _____ 17 _____
adjectives ending in consonant + -y	dry 2 _____	8 _____ happier	18 _____ 19 _____
longer adjectives (two or more syllables)	3 _____ difficult extreme	more fascinating 9 _____ 10 _____	the most fascinating 20 _____ 21 _____
irregular adjectives	4 _____ good far	11 _____ 12 _____ 13 _____	the worst 22 _____ 23 _____

3 **Complete the sentences. Use the superlative form of the adjectives.**

0 It's Cindy's birthday tomorrow. She's _____ _the happiest_ _____ (happy) girl in class.

1 Brazil is _____ (big) country in South America.

2 I didn't study for the test. That's why I got _____ (bad) grade in the class.

3 I think email is _____ (good) way of contacting people.

4 We all live a long way from school, but Sam lives the _____ (far).

5 She's great at math. She can solve _____ (difficult) puzzles.

Workbook page 83 ▶

VOCABULARY
The weather

1 🔊2.24 **Write the words under the pictures. Listen and check.**

freezing | sunny | rainy | humid | windy | wet | cloudy | dry | warm | foggy | cold | hot

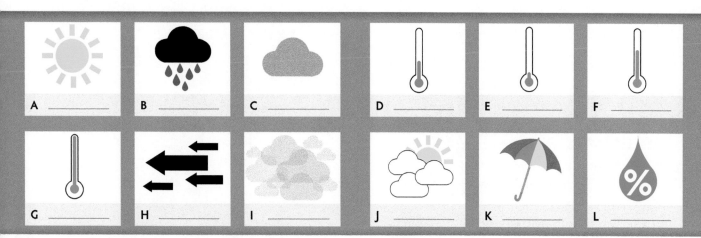

| A ___ | B ___ | C ___ | D ___ | E ___ | F ___ |

| G ___ | H ___ | I ___ | J ___ | K ___ | L ___ |

2 **Think about the different kinds of weather. In your notebook, write reasons why you think they can be good.**

a sunny day: We can ride our bikes.
a hot day: We can go swimming.
a rainy day: We can play computer games.

3 SPEAKING **Work in pairs. Make dialogues with a partner.**

What a nice day.

Yes, it's really warm. Let's ride our bikes.

Great idea.

Workbook page 84 ▶

The competition

1 🔊 2.25 **Look at the photos and answer the questions. Then read and listen and check your answers.**

What competition is Mr. Lane entering?
Why is Megan upset?

OLIVIA Hi, guys. Where's Megan?
RYAN She's not with us.
OLIVIA That's strange. I'm sure she said three o'clock.
RYAN Well, it's a nice day. Maybe she went swimming?
LUKE It's only a quarter after three now. She'll be here in a minute.

1

RYAN Hi, Mr. Lane. How are you?
MR. LANE I'm OK – a little busy with this Prettiest Park Competition.
OLIVIA Prettiest Park Competition? What's that?
MR. LANE It's a competition to choose the best park in the city.

2

MR. LANE We did really well last year. We came in second.
RYAN Oh! Good job!
LUKE But this year you want to do better.
MR. LANE Of course. I want to show the judges that my park is the most beautiful one in the city.
LUKE Well, good luck. I hope you win.
MR. LANE Thanks. It's a lot of work though, and I don't have much time. And no one to help me, either.

3

MEGAN Sorry I'm late.
OLIVIA No problem. Are you all right?
MEGAN Not really. I was at my grandpa's new place. He's pretty upset about having to move. He really misses his garden.
LUKE Does he like gardening, then?
MEGAN Like it?! He loves it!

4

DEVELOPING SPEAKING

2 Work in pairs. Discuss what happens next in the story. Write down your ideas.

We think they go to see Megan's grandpa.

3 ▶ EP5 Watch to find out how the story continues.

4 Put the events in the right order.

a Megan's grandfather meets Mr. Lane. ☐

b Megan and Luke go and see her grandfather. 1

c They admire the garden. ☐

d Megan's grandfather shows the trophy to Megan, Luke, Ryan, and Olivia. ☐

e Luke tells Megan's grandfather about the competition. ☐

f Mr. Lane and Megan's grandfather work in the park. ☐

PHRASES FOR FLUENCY

1 Find the expressions 1–5 in the story. Who says them? How do you say them in your language?

0 … in a minute. *Luke*   3 No problem. _____

1 Good job! _____   4 Not really. _____

2 … , either. _____   5 … , then? _____

2 Complete the conversations with the expressions in Exercise 1.

1 A I got 87% on the test, Dad.

B _____ ! Did you study hard for it, _____ ?

2 A Hi, James. I can't talk right now, but I'll call you _____ , OK?

B _____ . Call me back when you can.

3 A Did you enjoy the movie?

B No, _____ . I didn't like the book very much, _____ .

WordWise
Phrases with *with*

1 Complete the sentences from the story with the phrases in the list.

busy with | have to do with | with us

1 Megan? She's not _____ .

2 I'm very _____ the competition.

3 What does this _____ me?

2 Match the parts of the sentences.

1 You kill the lion ☐

2 It's a paradise ☐

3 Let's choose the hotel ☐

4 Are you good ☐

a with the biggest rooms.

b with your spear.

c with animals?

d with 200 different kinds of birds.

3 Complete the sentences with the phrases in Exercises 1 and 2.

0 He lives in a house *with* four bedrooms.

1 Sorry, I can't talk now, I'm _____ my homework.

2 We went to the lake and some friends came _____ .

3 I'm sorry you're angry, but it doesn't _____ anything _____ me.

4 Do you have a problem with your cat? Talk to John – he's _____ cats.

Workbook page 84 ➜

1

2

3

FUNCTIONS
Paying compliments

1 Put the words in order to make compliments.

1 a / garden / beautiful / What

2 wonderful / a / garden / It's

3 I / flowers / blue / those / love

2 Work in pairs. Use the photos to make compliments.

What a lovely picture!

10 AROUND TOWN

A

B

C

READING

1 Look at the photos. In which one can you see these things?

1 a **harbor** full of boats
2 a **castle** made of ice
3 a really tall **skyscraper**

2 **SPEAKING** Work in pairs. Name more places in a town.

station, park, museum, hotel

3 **SPEAKING** How important are these buildings for a town? Think about who each building is important for and why. Compare your ideas with another pair.

> *A hotel is important for tourists. They need a place to stay.*

4 **SPEAKING** Work in pairs. Discuss the questions.

1 What is the **population** of your town?
2 Does your town have a **festival** each year?

5 🔊 2.26 Read and listen to the blogs. Answer the questions.

1 Where are the writers living now?
2 Where are they going to live?
3 When are they moving?

6 Are the sentences "Right" (A) or "Wrong" (B)? If there is not enough information to answer "Right" (A) or "Wrong" (B), choose "Doesn't say" (C).

1 Alice's mom's job is for a year and a half.
   A Right   B Wrong   C Doesn't say
2 Alice is worried about getting bored in Dubai.
   A Right   B Wrong   C Doesn't say
3 She is excited to learn about Arab culture.
   A Right   B Wrong   C Doesn't say
4 It gets very cold in Yellowknife.
   A Right   B Wrong   C Doesn't say
5 The Snowking Winter Festival takes place on ice.
   A Right   B Wrong   C Doesn't say
6 Brian really likes sports.
   A Right   B Wrong   C Doesn't say

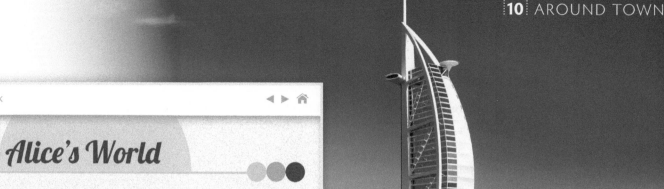

Alice's World

Today — rain in Seattle. Tomorrow — sun in Dubai! It's time to go. We're going to fly out tomorrow! I am soooo excited! OK, I'm a little sad to say goodbye to my friends, but we aren't going to be in Dubai too long. Mom's contract is only for 18 months. Actually, that's a pretty long time, but I'm definitely not going to get bored. There are lots of things to do in Dubai. Here's what I'm going to do:

- Go to the top of the Burj al Arab (you know — that building that looks like a ship's sail).
- Visit Port Jebel Ali — the largest man-made harbor in the world.
- Shop — there are zillions of shopping malls there. You can go skiing in one of them.
- Eat Middle Eastern food — I just love it.
- Get into khaliji music — it's amazing.
- Play some golf in the desert (yes, it's possible) and see some tennis at the Dubai tennis stadium.
- And go to school, of course. I'm going to go to the Dubai International School.

I think that's enough to keep me busy!

The Life of Brian

Big news this week. We're moving! That's right, two months from now it's "Goodbye Toronto" and "Hello Yellowknife!"

For those of you who don't know, Yellowknife (population about 19,000) is right at the top of Canada, so obviously it's pretty cold (minus 27°C in January!), but it gets up to 17°C in the summer.

We're going because my dad has a new job. He's going to work for a diamond company there.

Anyway, the best thing about Yellowknife is every winter there's this really cool festival. It's called the Snowking Winter Festival. Basically, every year they build a really big ice castle on the frozen lake. Then they have lots of concerts and activities for kids. They even show movies on the walls of the castle. I'm definitely going to that. It's also a really good place to see the Northern Lights. I promise to take lots of pictures and post them here.

My sister and I are going to go to Sir John Franklin High School. It has a really good theater program, so I'm going to do some acting there for sure. There's a good sports center, too. It's going to be different, but I'm sure I'm going to have a good time. And don't worry — I'm not going to stop writing my blog.

■ THiNK VALUES ■

Appreciating other cultures

1 **Imagine you are an exchange student in a new country for two weeks. Which of these things would you do? Check (✓) them.**

☐ Make friends with the local kids.

☐ Try to find other exchange students from your own country who are also there.

☐ Try to learn some of the language.

☐ Speak your own language (and hope people understand you).

☐ Look for TV shows from your own country.

☐ Read the books you brought from home.

☐ Visit museums.

☐ Listen to music by local musicians.

2 **SPEAKING** Work in pairs. Decide which of the things in Exercise 1 can help you find out more about a different culture. What other things could you do?

GRAMMAR
be going to for intentions

1 **Complete the sentences from the blogs on page 93 with the correct form of the verb *be*. Use contractions when you can. Then (circle) the correct words to complete the rule.**

0 I _'m_ going to do some acting there for sure.
1 He _____ going to work for a diamond company.
2 We _____ going to be in Dubai too long.
3 My sister and I _____ going to go to high school.
4 I _____ not going to stop writing my blog.

> **RULE:** Use *be going to* to talk about intentions for the [1]*future / present*.
> Use the present tense of *be* + *going to* + [2]*base form / -ing form* of the verb.

2 **Complete the table.**

Affirmative	Negative	Questions	Short answers
I'm (am) going to play.	I'm not (am not) going to play.	Am I going to play?	Yes, I [5]_____ . No, I'm not.
You/We/They're (are) going to play.	You/We/They [1]_____ (are not) going to play.	[3]_____ you/we/they going to play?	Yes, you/we/they [6]_____ . No, you/we/they aren't.
He/She/It's (is) going to play.	He/She/It [2]_____ (is not) going to play.	[4]_____ he/she/it going to play?	Yes, he/she/it is. No, he/she/it [7]_____ .

3 **Complete the future intentions with the correct form of the verbs in the list.**

~~not watch~~ | take | not fight | get | eat

Some family plans – to make us happier!

0 I _'m not going to watch_ so much TV.
1 My parents _____ out more often.
2 We _____ all _____ more exercise.
3 My brother _____ with me anymore.
4 I _____ the dog for a walk every day.

4 **Look at the table. Check (✓) the things you are going to do.**

tonight	this week	this year
do homework	play sports	write a blog
watch TV	visit relatives	go on vacation
clean your room	play a computer game	learn something new

5 **SPEAKING Work in pairs. Ask and answer questions about the activities in Exercise 4.**

Are you going to watch TV tonight? *Yes, I am.*

What are you going to watch?

Workbook page 90

VOCABULARY
Places in a town

1 **Match the places in the town with the people. Write 1–8 in the boxes.**

1 concert hall | 2 parking lot
3 shopping mall | 4 bus station
5 police station | 6 post office
7 soccer stadium | 8 sports center

2 **SPEAKING Work in pairs. Describe a place from Exercise 1 for your partner to guess.**

You go here to buy clothes.

Workbook page 92

LISTENING

1 **◀))2.27** **Listen to Tom and Annie. Who is Tom going to the movies with: Emily or Annie?**

2 **◀))2.27** **Listen again and complete the sentences with places in a town.**

1 Tom wants to take Annie to the _____ .
2 There's a new _____ on Bridge Street.
3 The restaurant is next to the _____ .
4 Annie is meeting Emily at the _____ .
5 Annie's relatives want to see the _____ .

GRAMMAR
Present continuous for plans

1 **Look at the examples. (Circle) the correct options. Then complete the rule with the words in the list.**

1 What *are you doing / do you do* tonight?
2 I'*m having / have* dinner with my dad. We'*re going / go* to a restaurant.

present | future | plans

> **RULE:** We can use the ¹_____ continuous to talk about ²_____ for the ³_____ .

2 **Complete the sentences. Use the present continuous form of the verb.**

0 I *'m going* (go) to Dan's party on Saturday.
1 Oliver _____ (not come) to my house this afternoon.
2 Sara and I _____ (do) our homework together after school.
3 We _____ (not visit) my grandparents on Sunday.
4 _____ your class _____ (go) on a trip next week?

3 **Complete the conversation. Use the present continuous form of the verbs in the list.**

not do | go | buy | meet | do | play

KENNY   Paul and I ¹_____ soccer this afternoon. Do you want to come?
OLIVIA   OK. Can I invite Tim? He ²_____ anything today.
KENNY   Sure. And what about your brother? ³_____ he _____ anything?
OLIVIA   Yes, he ⁴_____ shopping with my mom. They ⁵_____ his birthday present.
KENNY   OK. Well, we ⁶_____ Jack, Adam, Lucy, and Julia at the park at two.
OLIVIA   OK. See you at two, then.

▶ Workbook page 90

3 **◀))2.27** **Listen again and complete Annie's calendar.**

FRIDAY: *dinner with Dad*
SATURDAY: ¹_____
          ²_____
SUNDAY: ³_____

FUNCTIONS
Inviting and making plans

1 **Complete the sentences.**

Inviting	¹_____ _____ like to go to the movies with me? ²_____ _____ want to go to the movies with me?
Accepting	I'd ³_____ to. That would be great.
Refusing	I'm sorry. I ⁴_____ . I'm busy.

2 **Work in pairs. Take turns inviting your partner to do these things.**

watch DVD | go theater | play tennis
go out burger | come your house

3 **Think of three plans and write them in your calendar.**

Saturday	Sunday
morning:	morning:
afternoon:	afternoon:

4 **Walk around the classroom. Invite people to do things and complete your calendar.**

> *Would you like to have lunch with me on Saturday afternoon?*

> *I'd love to.*

READING

1 Look at the photos. What problem does each one show?

2 Read the letters and match the problems with the photos. Write 1–4 in the boxes.

A

B

C

D

Our Town:

1 Our town is a mess, and that's not good for tourism. I hate the litter in our streets. Why can't people put it in the trash cans? It isn't difficult. We need to educate people quickly. We need more trash cans and billboards saying "Don't litter!" and things like that.

We also need to punish people who litter. I think they should spend a day picking it up.
Charlie, 14

2 People always complain about the kids in our town. They don't like us hanging out at the shopping center. They say they don't feel safe. But we never cause trouble. We only meet up there because there's nowhere else for us to go. We need more things to do and more places to go. A youth club would be great. There are lots of empty buildings downtown. They could use one of them.
Mark, 15

3 The biggest problem in our town is the cars. There are too many cars on our roads, and drivers don't care about pedestrians. They drive really fast. Some of them don't even stop at crosswalks! I ride my bike everywhere and I just don't feel very safe, even when I'm in a bike lane. We can stop this problem easily. Let's get more traffic cameras to catch these fast drivers.
Pauline, 15

4 People like to complain about the graffiti on the walls of buildings downtown. They think it's ugly. I agree that a lot of it is. But if you look closely, some of this art is really good. Some of these people paint really well. Why don't we use them to make the town more attractive? I think we should create graffiti walls where these artists can show off their art. Maybe this will stop the problem of them doing it illegally.
Paris, 13

3 Read the letters again. Answer the questions.

1 What does Charlie think people who litter should do?

2 What does Mark think young people need in the town?

3 What does Pauline want to do to make the road safer?

4 What does Paris think will help stop the graffiti problem?

■ TRAIN TO THiNK ■
Problem solving

1 **SPEAKING** Work in pairs. Discuss the problem. Make suggestions.

The young people in your town aren't happy. They say there is nothing to do.

_____*have a music festival*_____

_____

_____

2 Think about your suggestions. What are the advantages and disadvantages of each one?

Suggestions	😊	☹
music festival	*young people love music / fun*	*noisy / messy / expensive*

3 **SPEAKING** Decide which suggestion you think is the best. Compare your ideas with the rest of the class.

> *We think a music festival is the best idea because all young people love music. It's also a lot of fun.*

GRAMMAR
Adverbs

1 Look at the sentences from the letters on page 96. Underline the adjectives and (circle) the adverbs.

0   They drive really (fast.)
1   We can stop this problem easily.
2   It isn't easy being young.
3   Let's get more traffic cameras to catch these fast drivers.
4   We need to educate people quickly.
5   Some of this art is really good.
6   Some of these people paint really well.

2 Complete the rule.

> **RULE:** To form adverbs, add ¹_____ to regular adjectives (e.g., *quick → quickly*).
> Delete *-y* and add ²_____ to adjectives ending in *-y*.
> Some adjectives have irregular adverb forms (e.g., *fast → fast   good →* ³_____).
> Adverbs usually come immediately after the object of the verb or the verb (if there is no object). *He plays tennis well.* NOT *He plays well tennis.*

3 Complete the sentences. Choose the correct words and write them in the correct form.

0   His car was really ___*fast*___. He won the race ___*easily*___. (easy / fast)
1   Her French is very _____. She speaks _____. (good / fluent)
2   Driving a car isn't _____. You need to do it very _____. (careful / easy)
3   We need to walk _____. I don't want to be _____. (late / quick)
4   I did my homework _____. I was really _____. (tired / bad)
5   He drives really _____. I get _____ in the car with him. (scared / dangerous)

Workbook page 91

VOCABULARY
Things in town: compound nouns

1 Choose a word from A and a word from B to make things you can find in a town. Look at the letters on page 96 to help you.

A cross | youth | traffic | graffiti bike | trash | bill

B wall | camera | can | lane walk | board | club

2 Complete the sentences with the words in Exercise 1.

0   Slow down. There's a ___*traffic camera*___ just ahead.
1   I really like that _____ for the new shoe store downtown.
2   Don't litter! There's a _____ behind you.
3   Don't cross the street here – there's a _____ just down there.
4   The new _____ is really popular. Lots of people are painting on it.
5   I ride my bike to school. There's a _____ from my house all the way there.
6   We go to the _____ every Friday night. I usually play table tennis and hang out with my friends there.

Workbook page 92

Pronunciation

Voiced /ð/ and unvoiced /θ/ consonants

Go to page 121.

Culture

1 Look at the photos. What do you think a ghost town is?

2 Read the article quickly. Where are these towns?

3 🔊2.30 Read the article again and listen. Mark the sentences T (true) or F (false).

1 Kolmanskop was once a very rich town. _____
2 The UFO buildings are a popular tourist attraction in Taipei. _____
3 Fordlândia became a problem because there was nowhere for the factory workers to live. _____
4 The Ford family made $20 million from the sale of Fordlândia. _____
5 They closed Centralia because of an accident. _____
6 It still isn't safe to visit Centralia today.

Ghost towns around the world

We build towns for people to live in. But what happens when they don't want to live in them any longer? All over the world there are ghost towns, towns where people don't live anymore. Here are a few.

In 1908, many Germans arrived in Luderitz in the southern African country of Namibia. They wanted to look for diamonds and they found a lot. With the money from the diamonds, they built the town of Kolmanskop. It had lots of beautiful buildings, a hospital, a school, and even a theater. But when there weren't any more diamonds, they left the town. These days the only things that visitors to Kolmanskop see are empty buildings and a lot of sand.

In 1978, a building company started building a vacation resort in the Sanzhi District of New Taipei City. For the next two years they built a lot of round buildings. They didn't look like normal houses, but more like spaceships. People called them the "UFO houses." In 1980 they stopped building the houses because there wasn't enough money. For 28 years the resort was a ghost town. In 2008 they demolished all the buildings. Now, all we have are photos of these strange looking houses.

In Northern Brazil, there is a ghost town called Fordlândia. In 1928, Henry Ford – famous for his cars – built a big factory there to make car tires. He also built houses for the workers. Unfortunately, the weather in the area wasn't good for growing the trees they

needed to make tires. In 1945 his grandson, Henry Ford II, sold Fordlândia. The company lost $20 million. The empty buildings of the town are still there today.

About 70 years ago, Centralia was a busy town in Pennsylvania, in the U.S. It had five hotels, seven churches, and 19 big stores. In 1962 a fire started under the town in an old mine. They spent millions of dollars trying to stop it, but that didn't work. It became too dangerous to live there, and everyone had to leave the town. These days a sign across the road to the town tells people to "stay out." The fire is still burning today.

4 VOCABULARY There are six highlighted words in the article. Match the words with these meanings. Write the words.

0   very expensive stones   _diamonds_

1   destroyed   _____

2   a company that makes houses   _____

3   a small vacation village or town   _____

4   you find a lot of it on beaches
    and in the desert   _____

5   holes in the ground from where
    we get substances such as coal,
    metal, and salt   _____

5 SPEAKING Work in pairs. Discuss.

1   Imagine you are going to make a movie set in one of these towns. Think about these questions:
    - What kind of movie is it? (horror, romance, science fiction)
    - What's the story about, briefly? (It's about a …)
    - Who is going to star in your movie? (It's going to star my favorite actors …)

2   Present your ideas to the group and vote on the best idea.

WRITING
An informal email

1 Read the email. Answer the questions.

1   Where is Emily going to spend her summer vacation?

2   What is she going to do there?

2 Find these expressions in the email. Use them to answer the questions below.

Guess what! | You won't believe it. | I can't wait.
By the way, … | Anyway, …

1   Which two expressions do we use to change topics?

2   Which two expressions do we use to introduce some surprising news?

3   Which expression means "I'm really excited?"

3 Look at paragraphs 1 and 2 of Emily's email. Match the functions with the paragraphs. Write a–d.

Paragraph 1: _____ and _____
Paragraph 2: _____ and _____

a   Describe the city   c   Ask how your friend is
b   Give news   d   Talk about your plans

4 What is the function of paragraph 3?

5 Which paragraph answers these questions?

a   What famous buildings are in Sydney? _____

b   What's your news? _____

c   How long are you going to stay in Sydney? _____

d   What's the weather like in Sydney? _____

e   What are you going to do in Sydney? _____

f   Where are you going next weekend? _____

6 Imagine you are going to spend your next vacation in a famous city. Write an email (100–120 words) to your friend telling her the news.
   - Use the questions in Exercise 5 to help you.
   - Use some of the language in Exercise 2.

To: luckyluke@email.com
Subject: Exciting news!

Hi Luke,

[1] How are you? I hope you're not studying too hard. Don't worry, there are only two more weeks of school. Anyway, I'm writing because I have some really cool news. You won't believe it. Mom and Dad are taking me to Sydney for the summer. Sydney, Australia! I can't wait.

[2] So I did some research on the Internet. It looks like a really amazing place. Of course, there's the famous harbor with the bridge and the Opera House, but there are so many other great things to do there. I'm definitely going to hang out on Bondi Beach. And guess what! Mom's going to buy me some surfing lessons. I'm going to be a surfer! We're going to be there for the whole month of August. It's winter there, but I think Australian winter is hotter than our summer. So that's it – my big news. What do you think?

[3] By the way, Dad says we're going to be in Bangor next weekend. Is there any chance we can meet up? Let me know.

Love,

Emily

CAMBRIDGE ENGLISH: Key

THiNK EXAMS

READING AND WRITING

Part 2: Multiple-choice sentence completion

Workbook page 61

1 Read the sentences about vacation plans. Choose the best word (A, B, or C) for each space.

0 On Monday we're _____ to Rio de Janeiro.
   A to fly   (B) flying   C fly

1 It's one of the _____ beautiful cities in the world.
   A most   B more   C less

2 The weather there is nice. It's usually hot and very _____ .
   A freezing   B foggy   C sunny

3 We're _____ to visit my uncle and his family in Brazil.
   A going   B go   C to go

4 I'm also a little scared because I _____ speak Portuguese.
   A can   B not   C can't

5 Mom says I shouldn't worry because my cousins all speak English very _____ .
   A well   B good   C badly

Part 7: Open cloze

Workbook page 89

2 Complete the text about Llandudno. Write ONE word for each space.

LISTENING

Part 5: Note completion

Workbook page 79

3 ◁》2.31 You will hear some information about a shopping center. Listen and complete each question.

White River SHOPPING CENTER

● There are more than (0) ___300___ stores.

● There are restaurants and a (1) _____ on the fifth floor.

● Parking costs (2) $_____ every hour.

● Buses take people downtown every (3) _____ .

● Stores close at 9:30 p.m. every day except (4) _____ .

My name (0) ___is___ Hugo and I would like to tell you about the town where I live. It's (1) _____ the north of Wales, and it's called Llandudno. That's probably (2) _____ unusual name for you because it's a Welsh name. Here in Wales we have our own language. I (3) _____ born here, so I speak Welsh really (4) _____ .

Llandudno is (5) _____ most beautiful town in Wales. Well, that's what I think. It's by the ocean, and we have lots of beaches. They (6) _____ sandy but have lots (7) _____ small stones on them. You (8) _____ swim in the ocean if you want to, but it's very cold most of the year.

There are lots of things to do in Llandudno. There (9) _____ parks, and there's a small mountain with a chair lift that goes to a café at the top. There's a really good concert hall, and lots of great bands play here. There (10) _____ a youth club that I go to every Friday night with my friends.

TEST YOURSELF

VOCABULARY

1 Complete the sentences with the words in the list. There are two extra words.

windy | crosswalk | lake | hall | mountains | can | island | lanes | cloudy | sunny | station | house

1 It's very _____ today. You can't see the sun at all.
2 We live on a small _____ . The ocean is all around us.
3 Mom and Dad are going to the concert _____ tonight. They're very excited.
4 It's one of the highest _____ in the world. It takes three days to get to the top.
5 It's so _____ that my hat just blew off my head.
6 Don't cross the street here. There's a _____ just up there.
7 It's easy to get around town on a bike because there are bike _____ everywhere.
8 I lost my dog! I went to the police _____ , but they can't help me.
9 Put your garbage in the trash _____ over there.
10 We went fishing on the _____ , but we didn't catch anything. /10

GRAMMAR

2 Put the words in order to make sentences.

1 going / She's / nine / to / me / at / call _____
2 Monday / We're / morning / on / leaving _____
3 homework / carefully / her / did / very / She _____
4 keys / I / I / remember / my / where / can't / left _____
5 the / It's / day / hottest / of / year / the _____
6 than / That's / mine / car / expensive / a / more _____

3 Find and correct the mistake in each sentence.

1 I speak badly French. _____
2 Soccer is the more popular sport in the world! _____
3 The present most I liked was a dress from my mother. _____
4 She plays tennis very good. _____
5 He's ten, and he still can't to ride a bike. _____
6 We are to meeting him at nine o'clock. _____ /12

FUNCTIONAL LANGUAGE

4 Write the missing words.

1 A _____ a horrible day!
  B Yes, _____ stay inside and watch TV.
2 A What are you _____ later?
  B Nothing. Why?
  A _____ you want to go skateboarding with me?
3 A _____ you like to come to my house for dinner on Friday?
  B I'd _____ to. Thanks. /8
4 A _____ what!
  B What?
  A Mom's taking us to Disneyland this summer. I _____ wait!

MY SCORE	/30
22 – 30	
10 – 21	
0 – 9	

OBJECTIVES

FUNCTIONS: talking about health problems; making predictions; sympathizing

GRAMMAR: *will / won't* for predictions; first conditional; time clauses with *when*

VOCABULARY: parts of the body; *when* and *if*; expressions with *do*

READING

1 Label the picture with the words in the list. Write 1–12 in the boxes.

| 1 arm | 2 leg | 3 mouth | 4 muscle | 5 finger | 6 foot |
| 7 ear | 8 eye | 9 toe | 10 hair | 11 bone | 12 thumb |

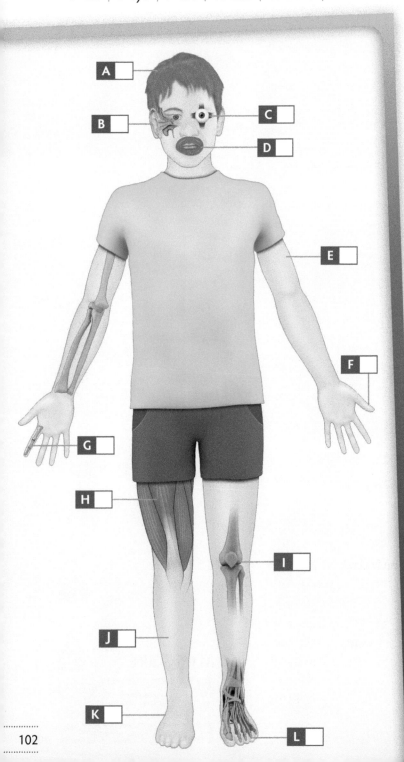

2 Write the words from Exercise 1 in the correct column.

Body	Face	Both
arm	mouth	muscle

3 SPEAKING Work in pairs. Discuss the questions.

Which parts of the body do you use when you:
- read a book?
- play soccer?
- watch television?
- make a phone call?
- eat a meal?
- walk to school?

> When you read a book you use your hands and your eyes.

4 Look at the picture on page 103 and the title. What do you think the article will be about? Choose one of the following.

1 What we want to look like in the future.
2 What the human body will be like in the future.
3 How we can change our bodies if we want.

5 ◀)) 2.32 Read and listen to the article and check your ideas.

6 Read the article again and answer the questions.

1 What is the most important reason why our bodies will change in the future?
2 Why will people be taller?
3 Why will people get weaker?
4 What will happen to our teeth?
5 Why will we have one less toe?
6 Why won't people have so much hair on their bodies?

Changing bodies

A long time ago, people were very different from the way we are now. For example, in really old houses the doors are usually much lower than they are today. Why? Because hundreds of years ago, people were shorter. Over time, the human body changes to adapt to a new way of life.

Can we expect the human body to change in the future? For sure. And the main reason is technology. It is changing how we live.

What kind of changes can we expect? Here are some possibilities.

1 Let's start with the example above. Humans are now ten centimeters taller than 150 years ago. So in the future people will probably be even taller. Most of us now have much better food than people in the past – and so we grow more.

2 We'll get weaker. Our muscles won't be as strong as now because we won't do a lot of physical work.

3 We are already using our feet less and our hands more (think about computers and smartphones and so on). So we can expect that our legs will get shorter and our feet smaller, and at the same time, our fingers will get longer. And our fingers and our eyes will both get better because they'll have to do more work together.

4 Now what about the mouth? It'll get smaller because technological improvements will mean that we don't need to talk so much – and also because our teeth will get smaller (so mouths don't need to be so big to keep them in).

5 It's very possible that people will have four toes, not five. The little toe really isn't needed anymore (people who lose them don't miss them), so it will probably disappear sometime in the future.

6 People won't have as much hair on their bodies as now because we don't need it to keep ourselves warm anymore.

Will all these things happen? And if so, when? These are questions that no one can answer for sure.

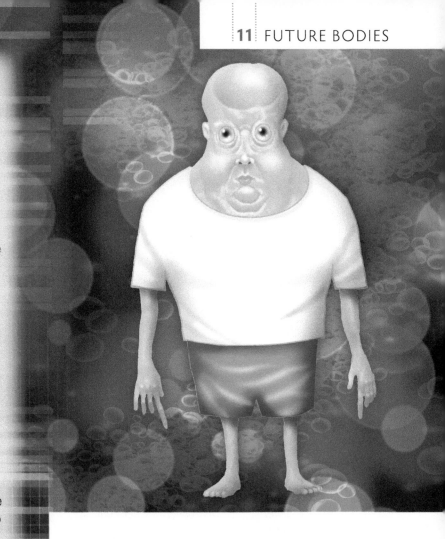

■ THiNK VALUES ■

Exercise and health

1 **Read the sentences. Give each one a number from 1 to 5 (1 = isn't true at all for good health; 5 = very true for good health).**

1 ☐ You should exercise often to make sure your muscles are strong.

2 ☐ It's OK to spend time sitting in front of the television.

3 ☐ Walking is good for you, even in places where the air isn't so clean.

4 ☐ Using a computer and writing text messages gives your hands and arms exercise.

5 ☐ You don't have to play sports to be healthy and keep fit.

6 ☐ It's a good idea to exercise anytime you can (for example, use the stairs and don't take the elevator).

2 **SPEAKING Work in small groups. Talk about health and exercise.**

1 Together, decide the number that the group is going to give to each of the sentences in Exercise 1.

2 Together, decide on and write another sentence that shows how the group feels about health and exercise.

3 Compare your ideas with other groups.

GRAMMAR
will / won't for predictions

1 Look at the sentences from the article on page 103. Complete with *will / 'll / won't*. Then complete the rule.

1 Our fingers _____ get longer.

2 They _____ have to do more work together.

3 Our muscles _____ be as strong as now because we _____ do a lot of physical work.

> **RULE:** Use ¹_____ (*will*) or ²_____ (*will not*) + base form of the verb to make predictions about the future.

2 Complete the table.

Affirmative	Negative
I/You/We/They/He/She/It ¹_____ (will) come.	I/You/We/They/He/She/It ²_____ (will not) come.

Questions	Short answers
³_____ I/you/we/ they/he/she/it come?	Yes, I/you/we/they/he/she/it ⁴_____ . No, I/you/we/they/he/she/it ⁵_____ (will not).

3 Complete the conversation. Use *'ll*, *will*, or *won't* and a verb from the list.

get | stay | go | see | give | do | help

ALICE The French test is tomorrow! I hate French. I'm sure I ⁰ *won't get* any answers right!

MARK Don't worry, you ¹_____ fine! You got a good grade on the last test.

ALICE Yes, but this is more difficult. I really don't feel well. Maybe I ²_____ to school tomorrow. I ³_____ in bed all day.

MARK That ⁴_____ you. The teacher ⁵_____ you the test the next day.

ALICE You're right. But what can I do?

MARK Look, why don't I come over to your place after school? We can do some French together. You ⁶_____ that it isn't so difficult.

ALICE Oh, thanks, Mark.

4 **SPEAKING** Work in pairs. Act out the conversation in Exercise 3.

> Workbook page 100

> ## Pronunciation
> The /h/ consonant sound
> Go to page 121. 🔊

VOCABULARY
Parts of the body

1 Match the words with the photos. Write numbers 1–10 in the boxes.

1 ankle | 2 back | 3 elbow | 4 knees | 5 lips | 6 neck | 7 shoulder | 8 stomach | 9 throat | 10 tongue

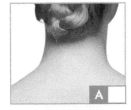 A
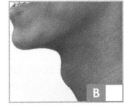 B
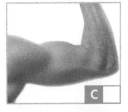 C
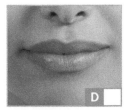 D
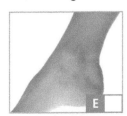 E

 F
 G
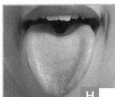 H
 I
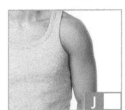 J

2 🔊 2.35 Listen and match the speakers with the pictures. Write numbers 1–3 in the boxes.

 A
 B
 C

> Workbook page 102

LISTENING

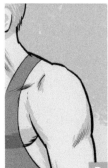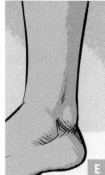

1 **Look at the pictures A–C. Answer these questions for each one.**

1 Who are the two people?
2 Where are the two people?

2 ◀))2.36 **Listen to three conversations. Match the pictures with the conversations.**

	Speakers (A, B, or C)	Problem (D, E, or F)
Conversation 1		
Conversation 2		
Conversation 3		

3 ◀))2.36 **Listen again. Mark the statements T (true) or F (false).**

1 Katie hurt her shoulder while she was watching skateboarding. _____
2 When Katie fell, it wasn't a bad fall. _____
3 David's ankle hurts all the time. _____
4 David's mother wants to take him to the doctor. _____
5 Sam didn't tell his parents about his back. _____
6 Molly wants to take Sam to see the doctor at school. _____

4 **Who said these things? Match the sentences with the speakers.**

1 ⬜ Are you all right?   a the doctor
2 ⬜ Does it hurt?   b David's mother
3 ⬜ What's the matter?   c Sam
4 ⬜ It hurts a little.   d Molly
5 ⬜ My shoulder hurts.   e David
6 ⬜ I have a backache.   f Katie

SPEAKING

Work in pairs. Choose one of the pictures in Exercise 2 (A, B, or C). Role play the conversation.

1 Decide who will be each person in the picture.
2 Choose a different part of the body from the conversation you heard for your picture (example: for Picture A, choose "head" not "back").
3 Have a conversation.
4 Now choose another picture. Change roles.

■ THiNK SELF-ESTEEM ■

Getting help

1 **Read and check (✓) the sentences that are true for you.**

⬜ 1 I don't like going to the doctor, so I don't go.
⬜ 2 If I have a problem, I don't like telling other people about it.
⬜ 3 If I don't feel well, I tell someone.
⬜ 4 I don't want other people to worry about me.
⬜ 5 It's OK to get help from people around you.
⬜ 6 It's important to go to the doctor if you often have the same health problem.

2 SPEAKING **Compare your ideas in class.**

3 **Who can you talk to about these problems?**

1 a headache   3 difficult homework
2 a problem at school 4 a problem with a friend

LOOK!

stomachache

earache

headache

toothache

READING

1 Read the posts. Write a name under each picture: Alyssa, Pete, Shanna, Julia, or Mike.

2 Read the posts again. Who talks about these things? Write the names.

1 dangerous things _____   4 eyes _____

2 making faces _____   5 a vegetable _____

3 making a noise _____

3 **SPEAKING** Do you know any more "crazy" things that adults say to children? Tell the class.

A _____   B _____

C _____   D _____

E _____

Crazy things that parents say to their kids ✕

Alyssa
Now that I'm eighteen, I can look back at all those happy days when I was a kid at home! And I remember the things that my mom and dad said to me again and again. For example: when my sister and I were making noise, my father always said, "If I have to come over there, you won't be happy to see me!" LOL. Did your parents ever say things like that to you?

👍 LIKE · COMMENT · SHARE

Pete
Oh, of course! My little brother and I loved TV, and we sat and watched it for hours every day. And my mom always looked at us and said, "If you watch TV all the time, you'll get square eyes." Well, we watched a lot of TV and our eyes are still normal. haha!

Shanna
You reminded me, Pete. My dad always said, "If you sit too close to the TV, you'll go blind." But he had another favorite, too (I think he was always worried about our eyes, for some reason) – he said, "If you eat all your carrots, you'll see in the dark." I really like carrots – I ate them when I was a kid and I eat them now – but I still can't see in the dark!

Julia
I always liked doing dangerous things – you know, climbing trees and things. And my dad said, "If you fall, you'll break your leg." And he always added, "And when you break your leg, don't come running to me for help!" I didn't understand the joke for years!

Mike
Nice one, Julia! OK, here's another one, and I think every child in the world hears this. If I was angry or upset, I always made a face, and my mom said, "If you keep making that face, your face will stay like that forever!" That's the only one I remember – but when I think of others, I'll send them to you!

GRAMMAR
First conditional

1 Match the parts of the sentences. Check your answers in the posts. Then complete the rule and the table. Choose the correct words.

1 If you eat all your carrots, ☐

2 If I have to come over there, ☐

3 If you fall, ☐

a you won't be happy to see me.

b you'll break your leg.

c you'll see in the dark.

RULE: Use the first conditional to talk about ¹*possible /certain* events and their ²*present / future* results.

If clause	Result clause
If + simple present,	3 _____ (*'ll*) 4 _____ (*won't*) + base form

It is possible to put the result clause first:
If you fall, you'll hurt yourself.
OR
You'll hurt yourself if you fall.

2 **Put the words in order to make sentences.**

0   see Jane, / If / tell / I / I'll / her
    If I see Jane, I'll tell her.

1   my parents / I'm / will / If / late, / be angry
    _____

2   I / bring it / I'll / to school tomorrow / If / remember,
    _____

3   you'll / Jake / come / If / you / meet / to the party,
    _____

3 **Complete the first conditional sentences with the correct form of the verbs.**

0   If Kate _____*gives*_____ (give) me some help, I
    _____*'ll finish*_____ (finish) my homework in an hour.

1   You _____ (not meet) anyone if you
    _____ (not go out).

2   I _____ (come) to your party if my mom
    _____ (say) I can.

3   If Ken _____ (not want) his ice cream, I
    _____ (eat) it.

4   Susan _____ (be) angry if she
    _____ (hear) about this.

5   If we _____ (buy) hamburgers, we
    _____ (not have) enough money for
    the movie.

ROLE PLAY Work in pairs. Student A: Go to page 127. Student B: Go to page 128. Ask and answer the questions.

Workbook page 101

Time clauses with *when*

4 **Read the sentence and answer the question. Then complete the rule with *will* and *simple present*.**

When we get to school, I'll take you to see the nurse.

Does the verb *get* refer to the present or future?

> **RULE:** In sentences about the future, we use the
> 1_____ form after *if* or *when* and
> 2_____ + base form of the verb in the main clause.

5 **Complete the sentences. Use the verbs in the list.**

finish | get (x2) | arrive | end

1   When I _____ my test results, I'll call you.

2   When I _____ home, I'll check my messages.

3   The party will start when my friend _____
    with the music!

4   When the game _____ , we'll go and have
    pizza.

5   I'll lend you the book when I _____ reading it.

Workbook page 101

VOCABULARY
when and *if*

1 **Match the sentences with the explanations.**

1   [ ]   **When I see Al**, I'll give him your message.

2   [ ]   **If I see Al**, I'll give him your message.

a   It is possible that I will see Al.

b   I know that I will see Al.

2 **Complete the sentences with *if* or *when*.**

0   I can't talk to you now. I'll call you _____*when*_____
    I get home.

1   **A**   What are you doing tomorrow?
    B   _____ there's a good movie playing, I'll
    probably go see it.

2   I'm not sure if I want to go to the party tonight.
    But _____ I decide to go, I'll call you.

3   It's too hot to go for a walk now. Let's go this
    evening _____ it's cooler.

4   You can watch some TV _____ your
    homework is finished and not before!

5   There's a big soccer game tonight. I'll be very
    happy _____ my team wins.

Workbook page 102

LISTENING AND WRITING
A phone message

1 **Mark (X) the things that you do NOT need to write down when you take a phone message.**

1   the name of the caller [ ]

2   the telephone number of the person
    who takes the message [ ]

3   the name of the person who the message
    is for [ ]

4   the telephone number of the caller [ ]

5   what the caller wants [ ]

2 🔊 **2.37** **Listen to a telephone conversation. Complete the message.**

Message from: 1_____

For: 2_____

Message: *she needs* 3_____

Please 4_____

Number to call: 5_____

The phone call

1 ◀)2.38 **Read and listen to the photostory and answer the questions.**

Why is Megan's father stressed?
Who calls Megan while she's in the park?

OLIVIA Aw, look!
LUKE Looks like they're having a good time.
WOMAN Jason! You stop that. Do you hear me? Stop it!
RYAN What did you say, Luke?
OLIVIA Well, we all know what that's like – your parents, yelling at you.

MEGAN Oh, don't, please! The last couple of days ...
RYAN What?
MEGAN Oh, my dad. He's really stressed. He has a big business meeting he has to go to out of town, tomorrow and Friday.
LUKE Something important?
MEGAN I guess so. I don't know.

RYAN Well, I think you *should* know. I mean, he's your father, right? Family and stuff.
MEGAN Yeah, yeah. Whatever. But I know one thing: He yells at me all the time. Everything I do is wrong.
OLIVIA Poor you.
WOMAN Jason! I told you – don't do that! If I have to come over there ...
MEGAN Just like that. Another few years and I can leave home! I can't wait!

OLIVIA Just think, Megan. You'll be a mother, too, one day. Then you'll remember this.
RYAN That's right. And when we're parents, we'll be just the same as our parents. Wait and see.
MEGAN Hello? Oh, hello, Dad. What is it? I'm in the park.
LUKE Tell you what, though. If our parents weren't ...
MEGAN Shh!! Dad, say that again. What? The hospital? Mom?

DEVELOPING SPEAKING

2 Work in pairs. Discuss what happens next in the story. Write your ideas in your notebook.

Perhaps Megan has to go to the hospital.

3 ◼◀ EP6 Watch to find out how the story continues.

4 Answer the questions.

1 What happened to Megan's mother?
2 When will her mother go home?
3 What is the problem for Megan's father?
4 Why can Megan help without going to school?
5 What does Megan say to the others is "the good thing"?
6 What does Luke mean when he says: "It's all ups and downs"?

PHRASES FOR FLUENCY

1 Find the expressions 1–6 in the story. Who says them? Match them to the definitions a–f.

1	I guess so.	a	What I want to say is …
2	I mean, …	b	I really don't care.
3	Whatever.	c	Here's what I think …
4	I can't wait.	d	Yes, but …
5	Wait and see.	e	You'll know later.
6	Tell you what …	f	I hope it happens soon.

2 Complete the conversations. Use the expressions 1–6 in Exercise 1.

1 A I'm going to see the new Ryan Gosling movie on Saturday! _____ !
   B _____ – we could go together, _____ , if that's OK with you.
2 A What are you going to give me for my birthday?
   B _____ . It's a surprise!
3 A You look so funny in that yellow shirt.
   B _____ , Alex.
4 A Can I go out tonight, Dad?
   B _____ . But don't be late back, OK?

WordWise
Expressions with *do*

1 Complete the sentences from the video.

1 She was doing some _____ upstairs.
2 I can do the _____ and everything.
3 Thanks. She's doing _____ , though.

2 Complete the sentences with a word from the list.

burgers | homework | cooking | well

1 Joe's upstairs – he's doing his _____ .
2 Did you do _____ on the test?
3 They do great _____ at this café.
4 Mom relaxes on Sundays, and we do the _____ .

3 SPEAKING Complete the questions. Then ask and answer with a partner.

1 Where _____ you _____ your homework?
2 _____ you _____ OK with your schoolwork these days?
3 Who _____ the cleaning in your house?

Workbook page 102 ➡

FUNCTIONS
Sympathizing

1 Complete the extracts from the story with the phrases in the list.

Poor you. | That's a shame.
I'm sorry to hear that. | poor thing.

1 MEGAN But I know one thing: He yells at me all the time. Everything I do is wrong.
   OLIVIA _____ .
2 MEGAN Oh, _____ . Well, she'll be home tomorrow.
   DAD That's right. Then a few days at home.
3 RYAN _____ , Megan.
   OLIVIA Me, too.
   MEGAN Thanks. She's doing OK, though.
4 MEGAN But it means I can't go out with you guys on Friday.
   RYAN _____ .

2 Read the situations. What can you say in each one?

1 You meet a friend. You know that your friend lost something important yesterday.

   Poor you!

2 You hear that Alex broke his arm last weekend. You meet Alex's brother.
3 Your neighbor says, "I feel terrible today – I think I'm sick."

12 | TRAVELERS' TALES

OBJECTIVES

FUNCTIONS: talking about travel and transportation; talking about life experiences

GRAMMAR: present perfect; present perfect with *ever / never*; present perfect vs. simple past

VOCABULARY: transportation and travel; travel verbs

A ☐

B ☐

C ☐

READING

1 Match the words with the photos. Write 1–6 in the boxes.

1 bicycle | **2** bus | **3** boat | **4** car | **5** plane | **6** train

2 Name other kinds of transportation in English.

3 SPEAKING Work in pairs. Ask and answer the questions.

How do you travel …
- to school?
- to stores?
- to the movie theater?
- when you go on vacation?

> I usually go by bike.

> Sometimes I take the bus. Sometimes I walk.

E ☐

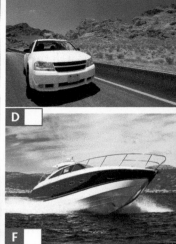

D ☐

F ☐

4 SPEAKING Work in pairs or small groups. Read about these people. For each one, say how you think they could travel.

1 An American family – a couple with two children – want to go to the UK on vacation.

2 A student living in London wants to go to Paris.

3 A businesswoman who works in a city is going to a meeting on the other side of the city.

4 Three teenagers in a city want to go to a party at a house that is five kilometers away.

5 Look at the photos and the title of the blog on page 111. What do you think the blog is about? Choose one of the following.

1 Someone who travels to many different places.

2 Different ways to travel.

3 Different places to travel in the world.

6 🔊2.39 Read and listen to the blog and check your ideas.

7 Read the blog again. Correct the information in these sentences.

1 Nora Dunn wanted to travel the world when she got old.

_____

2 Nora gets her money from some rich friends.

_____

3 Sometimes she writes home to ask for some money.

_____

4 She does the same job everywhere she goes.

_____

5 She traveled by boat to the Caribbean.

_____

6 She has appeared on television in every country she's visited.

_____

7 Life is always easy for her when she travels.

_____

8 She has a website to tell people how to spend a lot of money traveling.

_____

Ted's Travel Blog

HOME   ABOUT   NEWS   CONTACT

The non-stop traveler

Hello to all my readers. This week, I've decided to write about travel. Perhaps, like me, you've always thought that traveling is something for rich people. Well, now I think I've been wrong all this time. Why? Because I've discovered Nora Dunn.

Nora is one of a new kind of traveler – a professional world traveler. She travels all the time. Nora is from Toronto, Canada, and until she was 30, she had a business there. But then she made a big decision. Her dream was to travel the world – and to do it before she got old! So she sold her business and got rid of her belongings. And off she went.

Nora doesn't have rich parents or anyone who gives her money. And she doesn't have a high-paying job. But she's learned how to travel without spending lots of money.

Nora goes to a place and stays there for some time. She works to earn enough money to have a good time and to save a bit, then she moves on to another place. She prefers simple forms of transportation like trains or buses, but of course, there are times when planes are a necessity. And she writes from wherever she is, which earns her some money, too. She's done a lot of different jobs, including working in hotels and in restaurants. And she's learned things like cooking and meditation.

So, where has Nora been? Everywhere! She's been to five continents, and she's traveled to over thirty countries. All in six years! She's taken a train across Canada, and she's traveled by train from Portugal to Vietnam – an incredible

journey. She's lived on a boat in the Caribbean, and she's worked for her accommodations in Hawaii, Australia, New Zealand, Spain, England, Grenada, and Switzerland and a number of other places, too. And she's been on television shows in three countries. She's had a lot of fantastic adventures, and she hasn't stopped finding new things!

Some of her experiences have not been easy ones. In 2008 she helped people in Thailand and Burma after a cyclone hit their countries. And in 2009 she helped fight forest fires in Australia.

So she's seen a lot so far. She's learned that full-time travel doesn't have to be expensive, and she knows now that there are plenty of ways to do it – so many ways, in fact, that she's started a website to tell other people about them. It's theprofessionalhobo.com. I've seen lots of travel sites, and this is one of the best. Take a look. Perhaps you'll be the next "world traveler"!

See you next week.

■ THiNK VALUES ■

Travel broadens the mind

1 **Read what people said about Nora Dunn. Match the comments 1–4 with the values a–d.**

1 [ ] She's seen so many different countries, so she probably understands all kinds of people.

2 [ ] She's probably a better person now because she's learned so many things.

3 [ ] I think it's wonderful what she did in Burma with the cyclone and in Australia with the fire.

4 [ ] It's great that she's living her life without thinking about money all the time.

a helping other people _____
b self-improvement _____
c not worrying about money _____
d learning about other cultures _____

2 **SPEAKING How important are the values in Exercise 1 for you? Put them in order from 1–4. Compare your ideas in class. Say why you think the values are important or not.**

GRAMMAR
Present perfect

1 **Complete the sentences from the blog on page 111. Then complete the rule.**

1 Perhaps, like me, you _____ always _____ that traveling is something for rich people.
2 Now, I think I _____ wrong all this time.
3 She _____ a lot of different jobs.
4 So where _____ Nora _____ ?
5 Some of her experiences _____ easy ones.

> **RULE:** Use the present perfect to talk about actions that happened some time in your life up to now.
> Form the present perfect with the simple present form of _____ + past participle.

2 <u>Underline</u> **other examples of the present perfect in the blog on page 111.**

3 **Complete the table.**

Affirmative	Negative	Questions	Short answers
I/You/We/They 've (1 _____) worked.	I/You/We/They haven't (have not) worked.	4 _____ I/you/we/they worked?	Yes, I/you/we/they 6 _____ . No, I/you/we/they haven't.
He/She/It 's (2 _____) worked.	He/She/It hasn't (3 _____) worked.	5 _____ he/she/it worked?	Yes, he/she/it has. No, he/she/it 7 _____ .

4 **Complete the chart. Use the irregular verbs list on page 128 of the Workbook to help you.**

base form	past participle	base form	past participle
0 be	*been*	6 speak	_____
1 do	_____	7 eat	_____
2 go	_____	8 take	_____
3 see	_____	9 fly	_____
4 write	_____	10 swim	_____
5 meet	_____	11 win	_____

> **LOOK!**
> 1 *She **has gone** to New York.* = She is not here now – she is in New York.
> 2 *She **has been** to New York.* = She went to New York and came back (at some time in the past).

5 **Jack and Diane are 25 years old. When they were teenagers, they wanted to do many things – and they have done some of them but not all of them. Look at the table. Complete the sentences about them.**

	learn French	visit Paris	write a book	work in New York	make a lot of money
Diane	✓	✗	✓	✓	✗
Jack	✓	✓	✗	✗	✗

0 Jack and Diane _____*have learned*_____ French.
1 Diane _____ Paris.
2 Diane _____ a book.
3 Jack _____ Paris.
4 Jack _____ in New York.
5 They _____ a lot of money.

6 **Look at the information about Sue and Harry. Write sentences in your notebook.**

	visit another country	fly in a plane	swim in the sea	touch a snake	take a driving test
Sue	✓	✗	✗	✗	✓
Harry	✓	✓	✗	✓	✗

7 **SPEAKING** **Work in pairs. Say things about yourself and people you know.**
Remember: Don't say when in the past.

> *My mother has lived in Africa.*
> *I've won two tennis competitions.*

Workbook page 108 ▶

LISTENING

1 🔊2.40 **Steve Anderson is at his old school giving a talk about his travels. Listen to the end of Steve's talk. Mark the statements T (true) or F (false).**

1 He wants to get married and start a family. ☐

2 When he was younger, he didn't like staying at home. ☐

3 He's going to stop traveling soon. ☐

2 🔊2.41 **Now the children ask Steve questions. Listen and match the events with the places.**

1 ☐ The most interesting place he's been to.

2 ☐ The place where he ate a cooked spider.

3 ☐ The place where he was sick.

a Africa b India c Mexico

3 🔊2.41 **Listen again and answer the questions.**

1 Has he ever eaten a snake?

2 Did he like the spider that he ate?

3 Has he had any accidents in a minibus or taxi?

4 What do tourists and travelers take with them?

GRAMMAR
Present perfect with *ever / never*

1 **Complete the sentences with *ever* or *never* and complete the rule.**

1 I've _____ eaten a snake.

2 Have you _____ eaten anything really horrible?

> RULE: When we use the present perfect to talk about experiences and we want to say
> * "at no time in (my) life," we use the word [1]_____
> * "at any time in (your) life," we use the word [2]_____
>
> The words *ever* and *never* usually come between *have* and the past participle.

2 **Complete the mini dialogues with the words in the list.**

been | yes | eaten | have
never | no | ever | played

1 A Have you _____ seen a silent movie?
  B Yes, I _____ .

2 A Have you ever _____ to the Olympic games?
  B _____ , I've never been to them.

3 A Have you ever _____ tennis?
  B _____ , I have.

4 A Have you ever _____ really hot chili?
  B No, I've _____ tried chili.

▸ Workbook page 109

FUNCTIONS
Talking about life experiences

Work in pairs. Ask and answer the questions

1 ever / see / a snake?

2 ever / eat / something horrible?

3 ever / be / on television?

4 ever / speak / to someone from Australia?

5 ever / win / a prize?

6 ever / visit / another country?

> *Have you ever seen a snake?*

> *Yes I have. It was a python at the zoo.*

> *No, I haven't.*

SPEAKING

Work in pairs. Think of a famous person. Ask about things that the famous person has done in their life, and imagine the answers. Use some of the verbs in the list.

travel | stay | play | win | eat | see | drive | write

> *Mr. President — have you ever eaten fried spiders?*

> *Yes, I have. I eat them all the time.*

▪ TRAIN TO THiNK ▪
Exploring differences

1 SPEAKING **Work in small groups. Look at the pairs of things. Answer the questions.**

a What is the same?

b What is different?

1 A car and a taxi

2 A train and a plane

3 A vacation and a journey

4 A tourist and a traveler

The same: a car and a taxi have wheels / doors / a driver.

Different: you drive your car but a taxi driver drives the taxi. In a taxi, you have to pay.

2 SPEAKING **Compare your ideas with others in the class.**

> **Pronunciation**
> Sentence stress
> Go to page 121. 🔊

READING

1 Read the interview. Put the four questions in the correct places.

a Have you ever had any famous passengers?

b Have passengers ever left anything in your taxi?

c What's the worst part of your job?

d When did you start?

THE TAXI DRIVER

Meredith McIntyre is a taxi driver in New York City. She tells us about her work and some of her experiences.

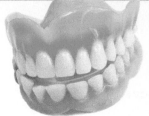

1 _____

I've been a taxi driver for about five years. Before that I was a tour bus driver, and I enjoyed it, but I wanted to be more independent. So I changed and started driving a taxi.

2 _____

Oh, yes. I've had movie stars, politicians, you know, lots of famous people. About a year ago, a really famous actor got into my taxi. I took him to the airport. There was a lot of traffic, and it took a long time to get there, so he missed his plane. It wasn't my fault, but when he got out of the taxi, he said some things that weren't very polite. I said to him, "Next time, take a bus!"

3 _____

Oh, yes! People have left all kinds of things in here – a suitcase, a hat, cell phones of course, even a dog once! Years ago, a woman left a pair of shoes on the back seat. And one time a passenger left his teeth here! Not real teeth, of course – false teeth.

People have also asked me to do some strange jobs. Once a doctor stopped me outside a hospital and asked me to take a skeleton to another hospital. And I did. But I asked the doctor to pay first – the skeleton couldn't pay, after all!

4 _____

Good question. I've always enjoyed being a taxi driver and I don't want to change. But of course, sometimes it's not great. I don't like driving around without a passenger, but it's better than just waiting at the airport or train station. I think that's the worst part – waiting.

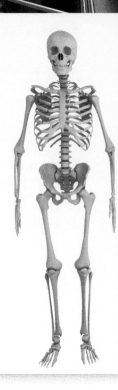

2 SPEAKING **Look at the photos. Say how each picture is connected to the article.**

> There's a picture of a tour bus. She was a bus driver before she became a taxi driver.

3 Read the interview again and answer the questions.

1 Why did she stop being a tour bus driver?

2 Why was the famous actor angry when he got out of the taxi?

3 Why did she ask the doctor to pay first when she took the skeleton?

4 What two things does she not like about her job?

4 SPEAKING **Work in two groups. Group A: you are bus drivers. Group B: you are flight attendants. In your group, think of answers to these questions.**

1 When did you start your job?

2 Tell us about an accident you've had.

3 Tell us about a funny moment you've had.

4 Do you like your job or do you want to change?

5 SPEAKING **Work in pairs – one student from Group A with one student from Group B. Ask and answer the questions.**

6 SPEAKING **Decide whose answers were best: the bus driver's or the flight attendant's.**

GRAMMAR
Present perfect vs. simple past

1 Complete the sentences about the article on page 114. Complete the rule with the names of the tenses.

1 Meredith _____ a lot of famous people in her taxi.

2 A year ago, she _____ a really famous actor in her taxi.

3 People _____ all kinds of things.

4 One time, a passenger _____ a pair of false teeth.

5 People _____ her to do strange jobs.

6 Once, a doctor _____ her to take a skeleton to a hospital.

> **RULE:** Use the ¹_____ to talk about situations or actions at a particular time in the past.
> Use the ²_____ to talk about situations or actions in the past when we don't say when they happened.

2 Find more examples of verbs in the simple past and present perfect in the article on page 114.

3 Circle the correct forms.

My name's Michael Edwards and I'm 26. ¹*I've been / I was* very lucky in my life because I have a good job and I travel a lot for work. ²*I've lived / I lived* in three countries: Colombia, Ecuador, and Peru. ³*I've lived / I lived* in Ecuador from 2012 to 2014. I live in Colombia now.

⁴*I've got / I got* married two years ago. My wife and I travel a lot together, and ⁵*we've seen / we saw* some wonderful places. Last year ⁶*we've seen / we saw* Machu Picchu in Peru.

⁷*I've done / I did* some cool things in my life, but the coolest was last month – ⁸*I've gone / I went* by bus through the Andes. ⁹*It's been / It was* really beautiful!

> Workbook page 109

VOCABULARY
Transportation and travel

1 ▶)2.44 Write the words under the photos. Listen and check.

~~a minibus~~ | a helicopter | a tram | a motorcycle
a scooter | a subway

0 _a minibus_   1 _____   2 _____

3 _____   4 _____   5 _____

Travel verbs

2 Complete the sentences with the correct form of the verbs in the list.

~~miss~~ | fly | catch | take | ride | drive

0 I had to walk home because I ___*missed*___ the bus.

1 I ran very fast, but I didn't _____ the train.

2 I have never _____ in a helicopter.

3 My brother has a motorcycle, and now he's learning to _____ it.

4 We got in the car and we _____ to Canada.

5 The rain was terrible, so we _____ a taxi.

3 SPEAKING Work in pairs. Ask each other questions. Use the verbs in Exercise 2 and the forms of transportation from this unit.

> *Have you ever flown in a helicopter?*

> *No, I haven't. Have you ever taken a tram?*

> *Yes, I took a tram in Toronto when I was on vacation.*

> Workbook page 110

Culture

1 Look at the photos and answer the questions. Then say what you think the article is going to be about.

In which photo can you see
- a student riding to school on a donkey? 1_____
- children walking to school along some train tracks? 2_____
- schoolchildren crossing an old bridge? 3_____

2 ◄))2.45 Read and listen to the article and say which country each photo is from.

Hard journeys for schoolchildren

"How do you get to school?" This question often gets an answer like "By bus" or "I walk" or "My parents take me by car." But not always – there are children in many different parts of the world who, every day, have to go on a difficult journey in order to get to their classes. They travel for kilometers on foot, or by boat, bicycle, donkey, or train. They cross deserts, mountains, rivers, snow, and ice.

These children in Indonesia have to cross a bridge ten meters above a dangerous river to get to their class on time. (The bridge fell down in 2001 after a very heavy rain.) Then they walk many more kilometers through the forest to their school in Banten village.

A

A pupil at Gulu Village Primary School, China, rides a donkey as his grandfather walks beside him. Gulu is a mountain village in a national park. The school is far away from the village. It is halfway up a mountain, so it takes five hours to climb from the bottom of the mountain to the school. The children have a dangerous journey: the path is only 45 centimeters wide in some places.

In Sri Lanka, some children have to walk across a piece of wood that connects two walls of an old castle. Their teacher watches them carefully. But in Sri Lanka, many girls don't go to school – they have to go to work or get married young. So girls are happy to take a risk in order to get to school.

B

In winter, the children of the tiny Iñupiat community in Alaska have to travel to school in extremely cold temperatures. They go to school and come back again in the dark.

These poor children live on Chetla Road in Delhi, India. Their homes are near dangerous train lines. Every morning they walk along the tracks to get to their school, 40 minutes away.

So, why do the children do this? It's because for them going to school means a better future. They hope to get a job and money so they can help their families and their neighbors. And this is why rivers, deserts, or danger won't stop them from going to school.

C

3 **Read the article again. What difficulties do children in these places face to get to school?**

1 the children who go to the school in Banten, Indonesia

2 the children who go to the Gulu Village Primary School, China

3 the children who go to school in Sri Lanka

4 the children of the Iñupiat community in Alaska

5 the children who live on Chetla Road in Delhi, India

4 **VOCABULARY** There are eight highlighted words in the article. Match the words with these meanings. Write the words.

0	from one side to the other	*wide*
1	do something that can be dangerous	
2	people living in houses near you	
3	a trip	
4	a group of houses usually in the countryside	
5	the things that trains move on	
6	very, very small	
7	not late	

5 **SPEAKING** Which journey is the one you would least like to have to do? Compare with others in the class.

WRITING
Someone I admire

1 **Read Mariana's essay about someone she admires. Answer the questions.**

1 When and where was her uncle Tim born?

2 Where does he live now, and when did he move there?

3 How does he travel in his work?

4 What does he want to do in the future?

5 Why does Mariana admire her uncle?

2 **Find examples in the essay of the word *in* with these things.**

1 a year 3 a city

2 a month 4 a country

3 **Look at the four paragraphs of Mariana's essay about her uncle. Match the paragraphs with the contents.**

Paragraph 1	a	what he does, and how
Paragraph 2	b	why she admires him
Paragraph 3	c	when and where he was born
Paragraph 4	d	why he does these things

Someone I admire

(1) My uncle Tim is a really great guy. He was born in Canada in 1980, in a city called Halifax, but now he lives and works in Cambodia. He went to Cambodia in 2014.

(2) My uncle is a doctor, and he worked at a hospital in Toronto for a few years. But in 2014 he decided to go and work in small villages in Cambodia because he heard that they needed doctors. He travels from village to village to help people. He has a small motorcycle that he uses. Sometimes, though, he goes in a very small plane because the roads aren't good enough.

(3) Uncle Tim says that he wants to stay there because there is a lot of work to do. He has also met a woman there — he told me in an email that they are getting married next July. Uncle Tim hopes that he can teach more people there to become doctors. He has learned a lot of the language — that can't be easy!

(4) I think my uncle is a great guy because he is helping other people and is happy doing that and because he has learned a lot about another culture.

4 **Think of someone who you admire: a famous person, someone you know in your own life, or someone you invent.**

For the person, think about:

- facts about their life (when they were born, etc.)
- what they do, where and how, when they started
- what they want to do in the future
- why you admire them

5 **Write an essay called "Someone I admire" in about 150 words. Use the example essay and language above to help you.**

CAMBRIDGE ENGLISH: Key

▌THiNK EXAMS ▌

READING AND WRITING

Part 5: Multiple-choice cloze   `Workbook page 53` ➤

1   Read the travel blog. Choose the best word (A, B, or C) for each space.

I love **(0)**_____ . I spend all my vacation visiting other countries. I never stay at home. So far I've **(1)**_____ to 56 different countries, and this year, if I **(2)**_____ the money, I'll visit three more: Cambodia, Vietnam, and Laos. It's a part of Asia I've **(3)**_____ been to, so I'm really excited about this trip. I want to make the whole journey without **(4)**_____ a plane. I plan to get to Thailand by boat and then **(5)**_____ buses to visit these countries. On the way home, I'll travel **(6)**_____ train through China and India, and then through Europe. It **(7)**_____ be a short trip – it **(8)**_____ probably take about four months. I hope my boss doesn't mind me taking some time off work!

0	Ⓐ traveling	B	travel	C	to traveling
1	A gone	B	been	C	went
2	A had	B	will have	C	have
3	A ever	B	always	C	never
4	A taking	B	riding	C	going
5	A travel	B	miss	C	take
6	A on	B	by	C	in
7	A isn't	B	won't	C	will
8	A will	B	is	C	can

Part 8: Information transfer   `Workbook page 107` ➤

2   Read the information about the school trip. Complete Gina's notes.

SCHOOL TRIP

Museum of Fine Arts, Boston
Saturday August 4th

Train leaves at 10:15 a.m. • Meet in station parking lot
$14 per person

School trip to the Museum of Fine Arts, Boston
Date ¹_____
Traveling by ²_____
Leaving at ³_____
Meet at the ⁴_____   about 9:30 a.m.
Cost ⁵$_____

Dear Gina,

Problems with the trains to Boston on Saturday. We will now be traveling by bus. It leaves half an hour earlier. Please now meet at the bus station 15 minutes before the bus leaves.

Everything else is the same.

Best,

Mr. O'Brien

LISTENING

Part 2: Matching   `Workbook page 61` ➤

3   ◀)) 2.46   Listen to Jack talking to a friend about his transportation project. How does each person get to school? For questions 1–5, write a letter (A–H) next to each person.

0	Jack	_F_	A	bike
1	Olivia	☐	B	boat
2	Mateo	☐	C	taxi
3	Brandon	☐	D	bus
4	Lauren	☐	E	car
5	Adam	☐	F	on foot
			G	scooter
			H	train

TEST YOURSELF

VOCABULARY

1 **Complete the sentences with the words in the list. There are two extra words.**

neck | trams | ride | scooter | helicopter | tongue | caught | back | stomachache | missed | lip | flew

1 He's really rich. He goes to work by _____ , and he lands on the roof of his office building.
2 I have a _____ . I think it was something I ate.
3 We _____ the last train home, so we had to sleep in the station.
4 Open your mouth. I want to take a look at your _____ .
5 I can't _____ a motorcycle, and I don't want to learn. I think they're dangerous.
6 I fell on my face, and now my top _____ is bleeding.
7 My dad rides his _____ to work. It's quicker than going by car and a lot cheaper.
8 We _____ over the mountains in a small plane. The views were fantastic!
9 I always sleep on my _____ .
10 Many cities are now using _____ to get people to and from work.   **/10**

GRAMMAR

2 **Put the words in order to make sentences.**

1 call / I'll / home / you / get / when / I   _____
2 taxi / I / train, / miss / If / the / take / a / I'll   _____
3 ever / Have / Europe / you / been / to / ?   _____
4 seen / She's / ocean / never / the   _____
5 different / five / lived / countries / in / They've   _____
6 grandchildren / be / easy / for / won't / our / Life   _____

3 **Find and correct the mistake in each sentence.**

1 She's played soccer yesterday.   _____
2 If we will be late, the teacher will be angry.   _____
3 I have ever broken an arm or a leg.   _____
4 I've never gone to the US.   _____
5 She has took a lot of photos on vacation.   _____
6 One day in the future people will living on the moon.   **/12**

FUNCTIONAL LANGUAGE

4 **Write the missing words.**

1 **A** What's the _____ ?
  B My leg _____ a lot.
2 **A** I _____ a headache.
  B I'm sorry to _____ that. Can I get you an aspirin?
3 **A** Have you _____ been to Canada?
  B No, I _____ .
4 **A** Do you think it _____ rain tomorrow?   **/8**
  B I don't know. I'm not _____ .

MY SCORE   **/30**

| 22 – 30 |
| 10 – 21 |
| 0 – 9 |

PRONUNCIATION

UNIT 1
/s/, /z/, /ɪz/ sounds

1 🔊 1.18 **Listen to the sentences.**

Gus makes cakes and treats. He works hard and sleeps a lot.
James enjoys all kinds of games. He plays a lot of soccer with his friends.
Liz's job is fun. She washes and brushes horses and relaxes by riding them.

2 **Say the words with the /s/, /z/, and /ɪz/ endings.**

3 🔊 1.19 **Listen and repeat. Then practice with a partner.**

UNIT 2
Contractions

1 🔊 1.27 **Listen to the dialogue.**

TOM	Here's your pizza, Jane.
JANE	That's not my pizza. I don't like cheese.
TOM	But Jane! They're all cheese pizzas!
JANE	No, they aren't. There's one without it.
TOM	You're right … it's this one. Here you are.

2 **Say the words in blue.**

3 🔊 1.28 **Listen and repeat. Then practice with a partner.**

UNIT 3
Vowel sounds: /ɪ/ and /i/

1 🔊 1.36 **Listen to the tongue twisters.**

Jill wishes she had fish and chips for dinner.
Pete's eating meat with cheese and peas.
Pete and Jill drink tea with milk.

2 **Say the words with the short /ɪ/ sound. Say the words with the long /i/ sound.**

3 🔊 1.37 **Listen and repeat. Then practice with a partner.**

UNIT 4
Saying -er

1 🔊 1.42 **Listen to the tongue twister.**

Jennifer's father's a firefighter,
Oliver's mother's a travel writer,
Peter's sister's a truck driver,
And Amber's brother's a deep-sea diver.

2 **Say the words with the -er sound.**

3 🔊 1.43 **Listen and repeat. Then practice with a partner.**

UNIT 5
Regular past tense endings: /d/, /t/, and /ɪd/

1 🔊 1.48 **Listen to the dialogue.**

MOM	What happened in the kitchen, Jack? It's a mess!
JACK	I started to make a cake, then I decided to make a pizza. I cooked all morning and cleaned all afternoon.
MOM	You cleaned? What did you clean?
JACK	My bedroom!

2 **Say the past tense words with the /d/, /t/, and /ɪd/ endings.**

3 🔊 1.49 **Listen and repeat. Then practice with a partner.**

UNIT 6
Stressed syllables in words

1 🔊 1.55 **Listen to the sentences.**

Sarah's funny, cheerful, and helpful.
Jonathan's generous, confident, and talented.
Elizabeth's intelligent, adventurous, and easy-going.

2 **Say the two-, three-, and four-syllable words. Stress the words correctly.**

3 🔊 1.56 **Listen and repeat. Then practice with a partner.**

UNIT 7
Vowel sounds: /ʊ/ and /u/

1 ◀)) 2.08 **Listen to the dialogue.**

LUKE   Let's look in this room, Sue.

SUE   Wow! It has things from the moon in it.

LUKE   Look at these cool boots! I saw them in our science book.

SUE   We should take a photo for our school project, Luke.

2 Say the words with the short /ʊ/ vowel sound. Then say the words with the long /u/ vowel sound.

3 ◀)) 2.09 **Listen and repeat. Then practice with a partner.**

UNIT 8
Stress in numbers

1 ◀)) 2.13 **Listen to the sentences.**

1 The next train to Austin leaves from platform three in **fifteen** minutes.
2 Your total is twenty dollars and **thirteen** cents.
3 Tomorrow is my grandmother's sixtieth birthday.
4 You can't go to that club. You have to be at least **nineteen** to go there.
5 There are **eighteen** people in my class, but there are thirty in my twin brother's class.
6 What? The concert ticket costs forty dollars? I thought you said it was **fourteen**!

2 Where is the stress on the red numbers? Where is the stress on the blue numbers?

3 ◀)) 2.14 **Listen and repeat. Then practice with a partner.**

UNIT 9
Vowel sounds: /ɪ/ and /aɪ/

1 ◀)) 2.22 **Listen to the dialogue.**

JILL   I'd like to live in the wild. What about you, Mike?

MIKE   I prefer a city lifestyle. I don't like lions or tigers – or insects!

JILL   But living in the wild's much more exciting!

MIKE   Yes, Jill – and it's more frightening, too.

2 Say the words with the short /ɪ/ vowel sound. Then say the words with the long /aɪ/ vowel sound.

3 ◀)) 2.23 **Listen and repeat. Then practice with a partner.**

UNIT 10
Voiced /ð/ and unvoiced /θ/ consonants

1 ◀)) 2.28 **Listen to the dialogue.**

BETH   Look – there's the theater.

HARRY   That's not the right one, Beth.

BETH   Well, it says, "The Fifth Avenue Theater."

HARRY   But we want the one on Third Street!

2 Say the words with the voiced /ð/. Then say the words with the unvoiced /θ/.

3 ◀)) 2.29 **Listen and repeat. Then practice with a partner.**

UNIT 11
The /h/ consonant sound

1 ◀)) 2.33 **Listen to the dialogue.**

DR. HARRIS   Who's next? Oh, hello, Henry. How can I help you?

HENRY   Well, Dr. Harris – my head's very hot!

DR. HARRIS   Let me see … does it hurt here?

HENRY   Yes, doctor! That feels horrible!

DR. HARRIS   It's your hat, Henry. It's too small!

2 Say the words starting with the /h/ consonant sound.

3 ◀)) 2.34 **Listen and repeat. Then practice with a partner.**

UNIT 12
Sentence stress

1 ◀)) 2.42 **Listen to the stress in these lines.**

car – plane – bike – train
a car – a plane – a bike – a train
a car and a plane and a bike and a train
a car and then a plane and then a bike and then a train

2 Which words are stressed in every line? What happens to the other words?

3 ◀)) 2.43 **Listen and repeat. Then practice with a partner.**

GET IT RIGHT!

UNIT 1
Adverbs of frequency

> Words like *sometimes*, *never*, and *always* come <u>between</u> the subject and the verb or adjective.
>
> ✓ I *sometimes do* my homework on Saturday.
> ✗ I ~~do sometimes~~ my homework on Saturday.

Correct the six adverbs that are in the wrong place.

I have always fun on Saturday! In the morning, I usually meet my friends in the park, or they come sometimes to my house. In the afternoon, we go often swimming. I never do homework on Saturday. In the evening, we have always pizza. My mom usually cooks the pizza at home, but we go occasionally to a restaurant. I always am very tired on Sunday!

like + -ing

> We use the *-ing* form of the verb after verbs expressing likes and dislikes.
>
> ✓ He *likes watching* TV.   ✗ He ~~likes watch~~ TV.

Find five mistakes in the conversation. Correct them.

LUCY What do you like doing, Jim?

JIM I love play with my dog, Spud.

LUCY Does he enjoy swim?

JIM No, he hates swim. But he likes go to the beach.

LUCY I like play on the beach, too!

UNIT 2
Verbs of perception

> We use the simple present with verbs of perception (*look*, *taste*, *sound*, *smell*) to talk about something that is true now. We don't use the present continuous.
>
> ✓ His new jacket *looks terrible*!
> ✗ His new jacket ~~is looking terrible~~!
>
> We use *look / taste / sound / smell* + adjective, NOT *look / taste / sound / smell* + *like* + adjective.
>
> ✓ This pizza *tastes awful*!
> ✗ This pizza ~~tastes like awful~~!

<u>Underline</u> the correct sentence.

1 a I think this jacket looks expensive.
   b I think this jacket is looking expensive.
2 a Your weekend sounds great!
   b Your weekend sounds like great!
3 a Look at that dog. He looks like happy.
   b Look at that dog. He looks happy.
4 a The music is sounding beautiful.
   b The music sounds beautiful.

Present continuous

> We form the present continuous with the simple present of *be* before the *-ing* form (e.g., *running*, *doing*, *wearing*, etc.) of the main verb, i.e, subject + *be* + *-ing* form of the verb.
>
> ✓ I *am looking* at the sky.
> ✗ ~~I looking~~ at the sky.
>
> But in questions, we use the simple present of *be* <u>before</u> the person doing the action, i.e., *be* + subject + *-ing* form of verb.
>
> ✓ *Why are you looking* at the sky?
> ✗ ~~Why you are looking~~ at the sky?

Put the correct form of *be* in the correct place in the sentences.

1 What you looking at?
2 They going shopping today.
3 I looking for a new jacket.
4 She wearing a beautiful dress.
5 Why he laughing? It's not funny!

UNIT 3
much and *many*

> We use *many* with plural countable nouns and *much* with uncountable nouns.
>
> ✓ How *many* sandwiches do you have?
> ✗ How ~~much~~ sandwiches do you have?
> ✓ We don't have *much* cheesecake.
> ✗ We don't have ~~many~~ cheesecake.

Read the conversation. Circle much or many.

SARAH Hi, Julian, do we have everything we need for the party?

JULIAN We have some potato chips, but we don't have [1]*many / much* fruit.

SARAH How [2]*many / much* apples did you buy?

JULIAN We have six apples, but we don't have [3]*many / much* vegetables.

SARAH I have four tomatoes. How [4]*many / much* people are coming?

JULIAN Everybody from our class is coming!

SARAH Oh, do we have [5]*many / much* juice?

JULIAN Yes, but we don't have [6]*many / much* glasses.

SARAH Oh dear! We have a problem.

too + adjective and (not) + adjective + enough

> We use *too* + adjective to say there is more than is necessary of something. We never use *too much* + adjective.
>
> ✓ The soup was **too cold**.
> ✗ The soup was too much cold.
>
> We use *not* before the adjective and *enough* **after** the adjective to say there is less than is necessary of something.
>
> ✓ The soup wasn't **hot enough**.
> ✗ The soup wasn't enough hot.

Mark (X) the incorrect sentences. Then write the correct sentences.

1 We didn't go because the weather wasn't enough nice. ☐

2 The sausages were too spicy. And the pizza wasn't warm enough. ☐

3 I didn't do my homework. I was too much tired. ☐

4 The food he eats is healthy not enough. ☐

5 The room wasn't enough big, and the price was too much expensive. ☐

UNIT 4
Possessive adjectives and pronouns

> We don't use *a/an* or *the* before possessive adjectives or possessive pronouns.
>
> ✓ This is **my sister**.
> ✗ This is the my sister.
> ✓ This is **mine**. Where is **yours**?
> ✗ This is the mine. Where is the yours?

Find five mistakes in the conversation. Correct them.

CLARE Hi Ben, is that your phone?

BEN No, it's a my brother's. His is black, and the mine's blue. The one on the table is the mine.

CLARE Oh, it's great! I need a new phone. The mine is really old!

BEN When is your birthday? Maybe your mom will give you a new phone.

CLARE Hmm. But the my birthday is in December! I need a new phone now!

Possessive 's

> We don't usually use noun + *of* + noun to talk about possession. We use name or noun + *'s*.
>
> ✓ That is **my cousin's house**.
> ✗ That is the house of my cousin.

Rewrite these sentences using 's.

1 She's the sister of my best friend.

2 They are the grandparents of my cousin.

3 Is that the brother of Thomas?

4 She's the sister of my mom.

5 That's the phone of my brother.

you, your, or yours?

> We use *you* to refer to the subject or object. We use *your* to talk about possession.
>
> ✓ Thank you very much for **your letter**.
> ✗ Thank you very much for you letter.
>
> We use *your* before a noun for possession. We use *yours* to replace *your* + noun.
>
> ✓ Is this **your phone**? ✓ Is this **phone yours**?
> ✗ Is this yours phone?

Circle the correct word in each set to complete the letter.

Hi Nadine,

Thank you for my birthday present. I got lots of great presents, but [1]*you / your / yours* was the best! I had a great birthday. All my friends came to the party and sang and danced and ate lots of pizza. I'm sorry [2]*you / your / yours* couldn't come! I know [3]*you / your / yours* birthday is next week. Are you having a party for [4]*you / your / yours*, too? I hope [5]*you / your / yours* have fun. Say hello to [6]*you / your / yours* parents for me.

See [7]*you / your / yours* soon.

Love

Grace

UNIT 5
Modifiers: *very, really, pretty*

Remember: we use modifier + adjective (+ noun). We don't use noun + modifier + adjective.

✓ Pompeii has **a lot of very old buildings**.
✗ Pompeii has a lot of ~~buildings very old~~.
✓ The buildings are **very old**.

Be careful when you write these words.

- We write *really* with two *lls*.
  ✓ Pompeii is **really** interesting.
  ✗ Pompeii is ~~realy~~ interesting.
- We write *very* with one *r*.
  ✓ Their house is **very** big.
  ✗ Their house is ~~verry~~ big.

Find six mistakes. Correct them.

We went to see our new house on Sunday. My dad wants to live near his office. It's realy annoying for me because a lot of my friends live near my house now. I was very sad when we went into the house. But when I saw inside it, I was amazed really! It looked pretty small, but inside it was really big. It had a kitchen really big and the bedrooms were verry big, too. But the best thing was the yard. It was beautiful really, with a swimming pool very big and lots of trees. I think my friends will like visiting my new house!

UNIT 6
Simple past (regular and irregular verbs)

To make any verb negative in the simple past, we use *didn't* + the base form of the verb. We don't use *didn't* + simple past. Remember to use the base form of regular and irregular verbs.

✓ We **didn't visit** the LEGO house.
✗ We ~~didn't visited~~ the LEGO house.
✓ I **didn't eat** lunch yesterday.
✗ I ~~didn't ate~~ lunch yesterday.

Circle the correct answer.

1 I'm sorry I didn't *come / came* to your party.
2 We didn't *went / go* on vacation last year.
3 I looked everywhere, but I didn't *found / find* my phone.
4 We visited the art gallery, but we didn't *see / saw* anything interesting.
5 We didn't *spend / spent* a lot of time in Paris. It was too hot!
6 I didn't *knew / know* you liked One Direction.

Double genitive

We form the double genitive with noun + *of* + possessive pronoun (*mine, yours, his, hers, ours, yours, theirs*). We don't use object pronouns (*me, you, him, her, our, your, their*) to form the double genitive.

✓ She's a **friend of mine**.
✗ She's a friend ~~of me~~.

We also form the double genitive with noun + *of* + possessive adjective (*my, your, his, her, our, your, their*) + noun + possessive *'s*.

✓ She's a **friend of my sister's**.
✗ She's a friend ~~of my sister~~.

Circle the correct answer.

1 Lisa is a good friend of *me / my / mine*.
2 Matt Damon is a favorite actor of my *sister / sister's*.
3 My brother went to the movies with a friend of *him / he's / his*.
4 I met a cousin of *Rory's / Rory* at the party.
5 She brought a new classmate of *hers / her / she's* to the party.
6 Isn't that woman a teacher of *your / you / yours*?

UNIT 7
have to / don't have to

> We always use the base form of the verb after *have to / don't have to*.
>
> ✓ *He **has to clean** his room today.*
> ✗ *He has to ~~cleaned~~ his room today.*
> ✗ *He has to ~~cleaning~~ his room today.*
>
> We use the correct form of *do + not/n't + have to* to say that something isn't necessary. We don't use *haven't to*.
>
> ✓ *You **don't have to** help me. I can do it.*
> ✗ *You ~~haven't to~~ help me. I can do it.*

Find six mistakes. Correct them.

I have to do a lot of housework at home, but I'm OK with that. I have to cleaning my room, but I haven't to vacuum the floor. My brother has to does that. We have to wash the dishes, but we don't have do the laundry. My dad does that once a week. I haven't to cook – my mom likes cooking. Of course, I have to doing my homework every day after school. I'm not OK with that!

UNIT 8
Review of question forms

> For yes/no questions, we always use the form *do + subject + base form of the verb*, except when the verb is *be*, when we use *be + subject + verb*.
>
> ✓ ***Does she live*** *in a big house?*
> ✗ *Does she ~~lives~~ in a big house?*
> ✓ ***Are you going*** *home?*
> ✗ *~~Do you going~~ home?*

Correct the errors in the sentences.

0 You have a big family?
  Do you have a big family?
1 Do you be OK?
2 Did your teacher lived in the UK?
3 You do have any pets?
4 You knew the answer?
5 Tom and his brother do go to college?
6 We meeting at 5 p.m.?
7 Didn't you liked the movie?
8 Your brother is coming with you?

UNIT 9
Comparative adjectives

> We use *more* + adjective with two syllables or more to form the comparative. We don't use *more* with adjectives with one syllable or with adjectives that are already in the comparative form (e.g., *smaller, colder, friendlier*).
>
> ✓ *His room is **smaller** than mine.*
> ✗ *His room is ~~more small~~ than mine.*
> ✗ *His room is ~~more smaller~~ than mine.*

<u>Underline</u> the correct sentence.

1 a Lions can run more faster during the night.
  b Lions can run faster during the night.
2 a The weather in the Kalahari is drier than in Europe.
  b The weather in the Kalahari is more dry than in Europe.
3 a It's more hotter in the summer than in the winter.
  b It's hotter in the summer than in the winter.
4 a People in the countryside are friendlier than people in the city.
  b People in the countryside are more friendlier than people in the city.

can / can't for ability

> We always use the base form of the verb after *can / can't*.
>
> ✓ *He **can swim**, but he **can't surf**.*
> ✗ *He can ~~swam~~, but he can't ~~to surf~~.*

(Circle) the correct verb form.

1 I love living by the ocean. On sunny days, I can *went / going / go* to the beach.
2 On warm days, you can *walk / walking / to walk* downtown and go shopping.
3 We can *learning / learn / to learn* a lot about wildlife from nature shows.
4 You can't *drive / driving / drove* a car if you're fifteen.
5 They can't *to come / coming / come* to the party because they're on vacation.

UNIT 10
be going to for intentions

> We use the present tense of *be* + *going to* + base form of the verb to talk about our intentions in the future. Remember to use the present tense of *be*.
>
> ✓ He **is going to study** all weekend.
> ✗ He ~~going~~ to study all weekend.

Complete the sentences with *be going to* and the verb.

1 He _____ (paint) his bedroom on Saturday.
2 I bought a new chair. I _____ (put) it near the TV.
3 We _____ (visit) my cousin because he's sick.
4 They _____ (go) to the stadium by car.
5 We _____ (watch) a movie tonight.

Present continuous for plans

> We use the present continuous to talk about plans for the future. We don't use the simple present.
>
> ✓ I'm **going to visit** my grandparents tomorrow.
> ✗ I ~~go~~ to visit my grandparents tomorrow.

> To ask questions about arrangements, we use question word + *be* + subject + the *-ing* form of the verb. Remember to put the words in the correct order.
>
> ✓ What **are you doing** tomorrow?
> ✗ What ~~you are doing~~ tomorrow?

Find six mistakes in the dialogue. Correct them.

LARA Hi Sam, what you are doing on Saturday?

SAM Well, in the morning, I play soccer in the park.

LARA What are you doing in the afternoon?

SAM I don't do anything. What are you doing?

LARA I paint my bedroom.

SAM Cool! What color do you paint it?

LARA I'm going to choose the color when I go to the paint store.

SAM Which paint store are you going to?

LARA I go to the store downtown at two o'clock.

SAM OK. I'll meet you there! Maybe I'll paint my room, too!

UNIT 11
will / won't for predictions

> We use the present continuous to talk about things happening now and plans for the future. We use *will* or *won't* + the base form of the verb to make predictions about the future.
>
> ✓ I'm going to a party on Saturday.
> ✗ I ~~will go~~ to a party on Saturday.
> ✓ I'm sure you**'ll do** well on your test next week.
> ✗ I'm sure you ~~are doing~~ well on your test next week.

Choose present continuous or '*ll* / *won't* to complete the email.

Hi Gareth,

I don't think [1] *I'll see / I'm seeing* you before my vacation. [2] *We'll leave / We're leaving* on Saturday morning, so [3] *I'm being / I'll be* very busy. [4] *I'll go / I'm going* shopping on Friday, so [5] *I'm not being / I won't be* at art class. [6] *I'll need / I'm needing* to buy some shorts – my dad says [7] *it'll be / it's being* really hot in Tunisia! [8] *I'll call / I'm calling* you on Friday night if I have time. I have to go now. [9] *I'll help / I'm helping* my sister with her homework.

Marcus

UNIT 12
Present perfect

> We use the present perfect to talk about situations or actions that happened sometime in the past.
>
> ✓ I **have met** a lot of famous actors.
> ✗ I ~~met~~ a lot of famous actors.

> We use the simple past to talk about situations or actions at a specific time in the past.
>
> ✓ A year ago, I **met** a famous actor.
> ✗ A year ago, I ~~have met~~ a famous actor.

Find seven mistakes in the text. Correct them.

My parents work for international companies, so I traveled a lot. I've lived in Europe, Asia, and the UK. Two years ago, I have lived in Spain for six months. My brother's only three, so he only went to Europe and he forgot that trip! My dad traveled to more places. He has been to Australia last year, but he never visited New Zealand.

STUDENT A

UNIT 2, PAGE 23

Student A

1 You are a customer in a sporting goods store. You like a pair of sneakers.

You want a black pair.

You want to know the price.

You want to try them on.

2 You are an assistant in a clothing store. Student B likes a sweatshirt. It's $36.95. You have green, blue, or red.

UNIT 5, PAGE 55

Student A

You and your friend have $200. You are at a street market buying things for a new room at your youth club. Here are the prices of some items:

- 2 chairs $30
- stove $20
- shelf $5
- table with 8 chairs $70
- desk and lamp $25
- sleeper sofa $75
- large carpet $70
- mirror $10
- dresser $30
- small carpet $30
- sofa $40
- 8 posters of movie stars $5

You want to buy the 2 chairs, the large carpet, the stove, and the posters.

You do not want to buy the shelf or the dresser.

You are uncertain about the table with the 8 chairs and the sofas.

Have a conversation and agree on what to buy.

UNIT 7, PAGE 73

Student A

You are a son or daughter. You are at home.

You want to see a friend.

You are calling your mom or dad about it.

When your mom/dad tells you that you should do some housework, ask what you have to do.

Also, tell your mom/dad that there are some things she/he shouldn't forget. When she/he asks you what things, say:

She/He …

- should buy groceries
- shouldn't be late tonight (you want to watch a DVD together with her/him)
- must not forget to bring some cookies!

The line is not good so you have to ask your mom or dad several times to repeat what she/he has said.

UNIT 11, PAGE 107

Student A

Ask your questions and answer Student B's.

1 What will you do if it rains this weekend?

2 What will you do if the weather's nice?

3 How will you feel if your teacher gives you a lot of homework today?

4 What will you wear if you go out to a party this evening?

5 What will you see if you go to the movies this week?

6 What show will you watch if you watch TV this evening?

STUDENT B

UNIT 2, PAGE 23

Student B

1   You are an assistant in a sporting goods store. Student A likes a pair of sneakers. They're $34.99. You only have brown or red (not black).

2   You are a customer in a clothing store. You like a sweatshirt.

   You want a green one.

   You want to know the price.

   You want to try it on.

UNIT 5, PAGE 55

Student B

You and your friend have $200. You are at a street market buying things for a new room at your youth club. Here are the prices of some items:

- 2 chairs $30
- stove $20
- shelf $5
- table with 8 chairs $70
- desk and lamp $25
- sleeper sofa $75
- large carpet $70
- mirror $10
- dresser $30
- small carpet $30
- sofa $40
- 8 posters of movie stars $5

You want to buy the table with the 8 chairs, the stove, the large carpet, and one of the sofas.

You do not want to buy the 2 chairs or the posters.

You are uncertain about the desk and the lamp.

Have a conversation and agree on what to buy.

UNIT 7, PAGE 73

Student B

You are a mom or dad. Your son/daughter is calling you.

Make sure he/she knows that he/she has to do some housework before he/she can go out. When he/she asks you what, say:

He/She …

- has to clean his/her room
- should load the dishwasher
- must not forget to vacuum

When your son or daughter tells you that there are things you shouldn't forget, ask what things.

The line is not good so you have to ask your son or daughter several times to repeat what he/she has said.

UNIT 11, PAGE 107

Student B

Ask your questions and answer Student A's.

1   What will you do if you stay at home this weekend?

2   What will you study if you go to college?

3   What will you buy if you go shopping this weekend?

4   How will you feel if your parents ask you to do a lot of housework this evening?

5   What video game will you play if you decide to play video games this evening?

6   Where will you go if you meet your friends tonight?